CONCISE

Microsoft®
Works
for Windows™

JoAnne Woodcock

PUBLISHED BY
Microsoft Press
A Division of Microsoft Corporation
One Microsoft Way
Redmond, Washington 98052-6399

Copyright © 1992 by Microsoft Press

Library of Congress Cataloging-in-Publication Data

Woodcock, JoAnne.
    Concise guide to Microsoft Works for Windows / JoAnne Woodcock.
        p. .cm.
    Includes index.
    ISBN 1-55615-493-3 : $12.95
    1. Microsoft Works (Computer program)   2. Microsoft Works for
Windows.   I. Title.
QA76.76.I57W658 1992
005.369--dc20   92-4619
                                                              CIP

Printed and bound in the United States of America.

1 2 3 4 5 6 7 8 9   RDRD   6 5 4 3 2 1

Distributed to the book trade in Canada by Macmillan of Canada,
a division of Canada Publishing Corporation.

Distributed to the book trade outside the United States and Canada by Penguin Books Ltd.

Penguin Books Ltd., Harmondsworth, Middlesex, England
Penguin Books Australia Ltd., Ringwood, Victoria, Australia
Penguin Books N.Z. Ltd., 182-190 Wairau Road, Auckland 10, New Zealand

British Cataloging-in-Publication Data available.

Acquisitions Editor: Marjorie Schlaikjer
Project Editor: Eric Stroo
Technical Editor: Dail Magee, Jr.

Contents

PART III: APPENDIXES

Note to the Reader

This book is your guide to Microsoft Works for Windows, a remarkably friendly application that can help you process any type of data—words, numbers, or sets of records—with ease. All you need to get started are a few basics, which you'll find early in the book. Once you're comfortable with Works you can, without much practice, turn your computer to many different tasks, from writing letters to balancing your budget, keeping track of names and addresses, even preparing mass mailings.

WHAT YOU SHOULD KNOW

Works doesn't expect you to be a computer expert; neither does this book. As the classified ads put it, you need only be "willing to learn, no experience required." You should have a nodding acquaintance with your computer and about the same level of experience with Windows, but those requirements mean little more than knowing how to turn on your computer, how to insert a disk, how to start Windows, and how to use a mouse if you have one.

The book starts off assuming that both Windows and Works are installed on your hard disk—that is, both programs have been copied from the floppy disks you purchased to the hard disk in your computer. If you need help installing Windows, refer to your Windows manual for instructions on running the Windows Setup program. If you need help installing Works, turn to Appendix A. The instructions there are brief, but they should offer all you need. You'll find both Windows and Works easy to install, even if you've never attempted such a feat before.

ABOUT THIS BOOK

Works is a collection of applications. A book cannot foresee which of them you'll want to use first or most often. What a book can do, however, is give you the understanding and skills you need to leave instruction behind and go confidently on your way. To reach this goal, the book is divided into sections, each with a particular focus:

- The introductory chapter, titled "Understanding Works and Windows," gives some training in Windows essentials. Turn to this information first if you and your computer are still relative strangers.

- Part I, encompassing Chapters 1 through 3, covers topics common to all Works applications—for example, how to open and close the documents you save on disk, how to customize Works to suit your preferences, and how to get help when you need it.

- Part II, comprising Chapters 4 through 10, is more task oriented. In these chapters, you'll see how to use the various Works applications—Word Processor, Spreadsheet, and Database—as well as associated mini-programs for drawing, charting, and creating database reports.

- The final section includes two appendixes. Appendix A tells you how to install Works. Appendix B lists and briefly describes a substantial group of built-in formulas, called functions, that you can use with the Spreadsheet and the Database.

When you finish this book, you won't know all there is to know about Works. Such coverage isn't possible in a book this size. But you will be comfortable with Works—it will have become just another familiar tool that helps you get things done.

ACKNOWLEDGMENTS

A book more or less begins with a writer, but it never ends there. Many other people contribute their thoughts and professional skills to the product that eventually reaches you. In this instance, thanks go to two special groups of people. First, Eric Stroo, editor; Dail Magee, Jr., technical editor; Ruth Pettis, principal typographer; Kathleen Atkins, principal proofreader; Debbie Kem and Barb Runyan, editorial compositors; Peggy Herman, graphic artist; and Lisa Sandburg, electronic artist. Second, but no less important, Libby Duzan and Tim Wood of the Works development group, both of whom kindly reviewed the manuscript. Together, these people deserve full credit if this book meets your needs, but none of the blame if it does not.

Personal thanks also to Kate and Mark, Kay, and "Skeet." Last in mention, they are first in everything else that matters.

Understanding Works and Windows

You've got a computer on your desk, and somewhere inside that computer is Microsoft Works for Windows. Now you can get to work. How? That's what this chapter is about. If you're not yet comfortable with computers or with Windows, this chapter helps you orient yourself and introduces you to Works. If you're already familiar with computers and Windows, skip to the heading "Starting Works" in this introduction, or go on to Chapter 1. If Works isn't yet installed, head for Appendix A.

WINDOWS, WORKS, AND YOUR COMPUTER

Works, as you know, is a computer *program*—a set of instructions that makes your computer do useful work. Collectively, programs are known as *software*—in contrast to *hardware,* the mechanical and electronic components that make up your computer system. Computer programs, like people, differ in the kinds of work they do. Some programs, such as Works, are *application* software; they help with result-oriented tasks such as writing, drawing, calculating, and keeping records. Application programs are far and away the type of software you'll rely on most often. They are not, however, the only type of software you use.

Within your computer you have two special kinds of *system* software named Windows and MS-DOS. These two programs take care of many necessary tasks that are constantly being carried out behind the scenes: reading the keyboard, displaying your typing on the screen, saving your documents on disk, finding those documents later on when you ask for them, and so on. Both Windows and MS-DOS are support software in the sense that they handle the routine activities that all application programs rely on.

Although you don't have to know anything about how MS-DOS or Windows supports your application software, you do have to know what they look like onscreen, if only to get your applications started. Computers can be set up to start in different ways. When you turn on your computer, you might see Works right away. On the other hand, you might see MS-DOS first, or you might see Windows. If Works does not appear automatically, what you see at startup determines how you get to Works.

MS-DOS

The MS-DOS *operating system* is the software that takes care of very basic computer needs. If Windows starts whenever you boot your computer, all you see of MS-DOS are some messages that appear on your screen but require no response from you. If Windows does not start automatically, startup ends with something like this:

```
C:\>_
```

The C:\> part of this line is the MS-DOS *prompt,* and the blinking underline that follows is the *cursor.* The MS-DOS prompt can be set to appear in many different ways, but what you see here is its usual form on a computer with a hard disk. The cursor calls your attention to the place onscreen at which the next character you type will appear.

If the MS-DOS prompt appears at startup, your next step on the road to Works is to start Windows. You do this by typing an abbreviated form of Windows' name:

```
C:\>win
```

and then pressing Enter.

WINDOWS

Whether it appears whenever you start your computer or only when you enter *win,* Windows takes over from MS-DOS. Windows is not quite an operating system, nor is it application software. It's an in-between type of program, often called an *operating environment,* that provides a consistent, predictable arena in which you, Works, and other Windows programs can function comfortably.

On the surface, Windows is a pleasant, easy-to-use, *graphical user interface,* or GUI (pronounced "gooey"), that sits between you and MS-DOS and helps make your computer work easier and more intuitive than it would be if you communicated directly with MS-DOS via typed commands.

Underneath, where you can't see it, however, Windows is much more than a friendly face for MS-DOS. It's a facilitator that helps software use computer memory efficiently, helps your computer run several programs at the same time, and helps Windows programs—those created specifically for the Windows environment—swap information seamlessly and with far fewer problems than non-Windows programs can.

In addition, the skills and concepts you learn when you use Windows also apply to your work with Windows programs. As a result, you can become proficient with Windows programs in a relatively short amount of time.

Your first view of Windows normally looks something like Figure I-1. Note the labels and what they describe. Windows is easy to use, but it does present you with a few new terms to learn.

As you can see, Windows draws an onscreen display more or less resembling an electronic desktop. The items on your desktop appear in rectangular, bordered *windows.* If a window is too small for you to see everything it contains, Windows creates *scroll bars* along the right and bottom edges of the window. If you have a mouse, you can click in the scroll bars to "pan" sideways or up and down to view other items.

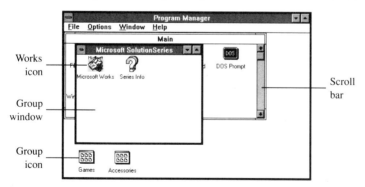

FIGURE I-1. *The Program Manager window is generally your first view of Windows.*

The main window you see in Figure I-1 belongs to the Program Manager—a "supervisory" program that helps you organize and run Windows programs, such as Works. Unless Windows has been modified to run differently, it normally shows the Program Manager at startup.

Within its window, the Program Manager displays *program groups*—sets of related programs—in either of two ways: as *group windows,* such as the one titled Microsoft SolutionSeries in Figure I-1, or as *group icons,* such as those labeled Games and Accessories. Like Chinese boxes nested inside other boxes, group windows and group icons are, in essence, windows within a window within Windows. Both contain programs you can run. The only real difference between them is that a group window is "open" to show the programs it contains, and a group icon is "closed"—it's *minimized* to keep it out of the way. The SolutionSeries group window in the figure contains *program icons* for Microsoft Works and Series Info.

You can open a program group whenever you want by double-clicking on its icon with the mouse. Similarly, once a program's own icon is visible, you can start the program by pointing to the icon and, again, double-clicking.

Making It Without a Mouse

Except for keyboard shortcuts, this book gives precedence to instructions based on mouse actions. Although a mouse is not strictly necessary, both Works and Windows are much easier to use with one than without one. If you're seriously averse to these little electronic rodents, however, you can ask Windows for tips on using the keyboard. If you have Windows version 3.0, press Alt and the H key (Alt-H), and then press K—shown underlined in the menu command Keyboard. (If you are using another version of Windows, press Alt-H, followed by the underlined letter of the topic you want to see.)

Whichever method you use, a Help window will open on your screen. Choose an item by pressing the Tab key until a topic you want to see is highlighted, and then press Enter. Once the topic is displayed, use the up and down direction keys to view the text. When you finish with a topic, you can return to the original list by pressing Alt-B until the list reappears. Press Alt-F4 to close the Help window.

STARTING WORKS

One of potentially dozens of types of application programs you might choose to use, Works is the type of application known as *integrated* software. That means it is a single program that uses a single basic set of commands, yet offers the functionality of more than one application. For that reason, one easy-to-use and easy-to-learn package can give you the capabilities of a word processor (for writing), a spreadsheet (for working with numbers), and a database (for keeping track of records).

To start Works from Windows:

1. Find the onscreen window titled Microsoft SolutionSeries.

2. Double-click on the Microsoft Works icon:

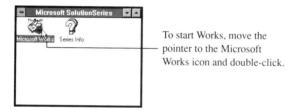

To start Works, move the pointer to the Microsoft Works icon and double-click.

In a short while, the Works application window appears, like the one shown in Figure I-2 on page xii. Once again, study the labeled items in the illustration—they tell you a lot about Works.

NOTE: *If Works is newly installed on your computer, this screen might be preceded by one containing a dialog box titled Welcome to Microsoft Works. Use your mouse to click the Start Works Now button, or press W, to advance to the startup screen.*

If Works is your first Windows-based program, you might be somewhat surprised by the number of buttons, bars, and assorted labels in the preceding illustration. Take your time examining them. Because Works is a picture-based, or *graphical,* Windows program, it uses many of the same techniques and onscreen controls that Windows uses, and for the same reason: to help you learn easily and work efficiently, especially if you have a mouse.

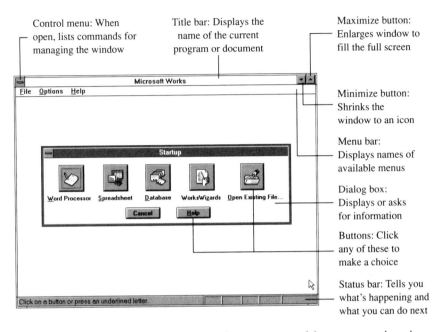

Control menu: When open, lists commands for managing the window

Title bar: Displays the name of the current program or document

Maximize button: Enlarges window to fill the full screen

Minimize button: Shrinks the window to an icon

Menu bar: Displays names of available menus

Dialog box: Displays or asks for information

Buttons: Click any of these to make a choice

Status bar: Tells you what's happening and what you can do next

FIGURE I-2. *The Works application window relies upon many of the same controls and techniques that Windows uses.*

What Happens If...

What happens if you want to start Works but can't see the Works icon or even the SolutionSeries window? First of all, relax. Remember that the Program Manager shows program groups both as group windows and as group icons. The Works icon disappears when you reduce the SolutionSeries window to an icon by clicking its minimize button. When minimized, the SolutionSeries window becomes a group icon like this:

To restore the SolutionSeries window and redisplay the Works icon, double-click on the SolutionSeries group icon.

Now, suppose you can't see the SolutionSeries window or its group icon. This can happen when you've been working with another Windows program, because Windows always displays the *active window*—the one you're working with—on top of any others you've opened. So, for example, if you've been occupying some idle time calculating your bowling handicap, the Accessories window might be concealing the SolutionSeries window.

- If part of the SolutionSeries window is visible, place the mouse pointer anywhere in the exposed area and click the left button. Clicking in any part of a window tells Windows to place it on top of any others. When the SolutionSeries window appears, double-click on the Works icon to start the program.

- If no part of the SolutionSeries window is visible, tell Windows to find it for you:

  1. Point to the word *Window* in the menu bar just below the Program Manager's title bar:

  2. Click the left mouse button. As soon as you do, a menu drops down. In the lower portion of the menu, you see a numbered list of group windows, among them the Microsoft SolutionSeries. Click on the name, and that group immediately appears at the forefront of your Windows desktop.

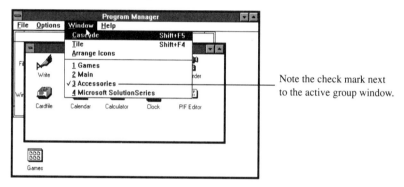

Note the check mark next to the active group window.

  3. Double-click on the Works icon to start Works.

CHOOSING WHAT TO DO

Recall that when you start Works it displays a Startup dialog box. This box, shown in Figure I-2, contains a number of buttons you can click to tell Works what you want to do next. (In fact, you *must* choose one of the buttons in the dialog box; you can't choose another menu item or even quit Works until you make a choice!)

To "push" a button, point to it and click the left mouse button. The table on the next page explains what the buttons in the dialog box do.

Starts the Word Processor with a blank screen on which to create any written document you choose.

 Starts the Spreadsheet with an electronic version of a blank ledger sheet.

 Starts the Database with a blank screen on which you can design a form for entering names, addresses, and other records.

 Opens the door to the WorksWizards—special Works tools that take all the guesswork out of creating an address book, a form letter, or a mailing list.

 Helps you return to a document you created and saved at another time. Choosing the Open Existing File button produces a dialog box showing the names of previously saved files and existing directories (file groupings). Chapter 2 tells you more about this option.

 Closes the dialog box but leaves you in Works. To start a Works application or open a particular document, you can then use the File menu. Chapter 2 tells you how to do this, too.

 Takes you to *online Help,* a comprehensive collection of topics that you can call up and view onscreen. Online Help is always available when you're using Works, and you can request it whenever you're stuck. You'll find out about Help in Chapter 3.

The Works Window

Although details vary from one Works application to another, Works is remarkably consistent in maintaining a predictable onscreen appearance, no matter what you're doing. Figure I-3 shows a typical Works window (here, the Word Processor).

As you might expect, Works has a "Windows look" and uses some Windows elements. For example, every Works window has a control menu, maximize and minimize buttons, and a title bar. (If you can't identify these in the illustration, see Figure I-2.)

The application window is, of course, the window in which Works runs—the one that contains the menu bar. Within the application window is a smaller *document window* in which you create, view, and modify documents, such as letters, budgets, and price lists. When you use Works, you can click the maximize button in the application window, the one in the document window, or both to enlarge the windows and take full advantage of your onscreen "real estate." When you maximize a document window, the document title is appended (in square brackets) to the application title.

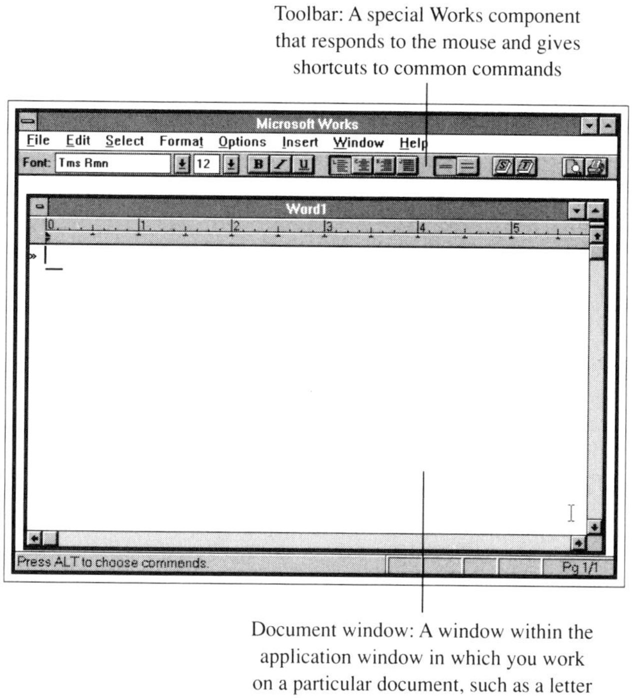

Toolbar: A special Works component
that responds to the mouse and gives
shortcuts to common commands

Document window: A window within the
application window in which you work
on a particular document, such as a letter

FIGURE I-3. *Individual document windows appear within the Works application window. The Toolbar is part of the application window.*

The Toolbar

Because you do more with Works than start programs and manipulate windows, Works also offers some graphical tools of its own, among them the *Toolbar,* illustrated in Figure I-3. The Toolbar appears below the menu bar, no matter which of the Works applications you're using. Designed exclusively for use with a mouse, the Toolbar contains a set of buttons that serve as shortcuts to common activities in each application.

Some Toolbar buttons remain the same from one Works application to another. For instance, the Toolbar always contains buttons to help you preview and print your work because those tasks are equally relevant whether you're working on a letter, a budget, or an inventory. Other buttons, however, appear only if they're appropriate to a particular type of work.

■ In the Word Processor, the Toolbar contains special buttons that can help you double-space your text, align paragraphs just the way you want, and even check your spelling or look up synonyms.

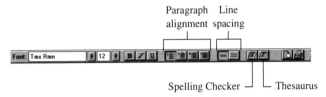

■ In the Spreadsheet, Toolbar buttons specific to the Word Processor are replaced by buttons that can turn plain numbers into currency values or percents, insert commas every three places in large numbers, add figures for you, and even turn selected values into illustrative charts.

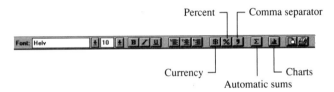

■ In the Database, the Toolbar changes again. Certain buttons make it easy to create a database (Form view), survey it (List view), display selected items in it (Query view) and, if you want, turn your records into a printable report (Report view).

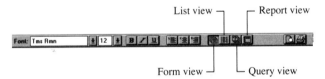

Regardless of the buttons it contains, the Toolbar always keeps the same basic appearance, and you always use it in the same way: by clicking the button you want. Don't bother trying to memorize any further details about the Toolbar here. Later chapters, in particular Chapters 4 through 9, describe the Toolbar's features in much more detail.

CHAPTER 1

Of Works and Working

No matter what type of work you do, you'll do it better if you know what resources are available to you and how best to use them.

The same pronouncement holds when you use a computer. As responsive as the machine is, it simply can't think. Although it (or rather its software) can produce a beep and refuse to act when you ask the impossible, neither the computer nor the software can tell you whether a word processor or a spreadsheet would be more appropriate for the book you want to write or the budget you want to prepare. To work easily and confidently at your computer, you must know what resources are available.

To help you develop an understanding of what Works is and what, roughly, it can do, the first half of this chapter takes you on a quick tour of the Works applications. You'll find sample documents and descriptions of the work best suited to the word processor, the spreadsheet, and the database. The second half covers some background information you need for putting Works through its paces. Essentially, this chapter is your equivalent of a planetary fly-by in a spaceship: It's an overview, a surveillance run. In later chapters, you'll land and begin probing the terrain in detail.

WORKS AS A WHOLE

Unlike most applications, which focus on a single type of activity, Works, as integrated software, spreads its capabilities across several different sorts of work. Like an all-terrain vehicle or a Swiss army knife, Works is an all-purpose, go anywhere, do (nearly) anything product—the blue jeans of software fashion.

The Parts of Works

The three Works tools—Word Processor, Spreadsheet, and Database—help with the most common tasks for which people use computers.

The tasks are common, but they are considerably different:

- The Word Processor is for writing: letters, reports, poetry, essays, diaries—any type of document in which words play the starring role.

- The Spreadsheet is for numbers, statistics, and tabular material: budgets, sales figures, corporate growth data, the national deficit—any type of document in which numbers have a tale to tell.

- The Database is for organizing facts of any kind: names and addresses, warehouse inventories, videotape collections, dinosaur bones, baseball cards—any type of recordkeeping in which organizing and retrieving data are your primary goals.

These three applications, the Works *tools*, are impressive enough, but there's more. While you're using the Word Processor, you also have access to a drawing program you can use to embellish your text with illustrations, logos, monograms, banner headlines, and other artistic touches. And while you're using the Spreadsheet, you can easily jump into a charting program that can turn rows or columns of figures into charts and graphs like those you often see in newspapers and advertisements. Finally, you can move from the Database proper into a reporting module in which you can design layouts for data records you want to print.

Running Works

Given all these capabilities, you might wonder how you're supposed to use Works. Is there a certain order in which you run these applications? Do you have to quit one to use another? Do you have to try to remember what you've done? In a word, no. No to all these questions. When you use Works, you can

- Use the Word Processor, the Spreadsheet, or the Database whenever you want, any time you are using Works

- Run any of these programs by itself, as if it were a single, *stand-alone* application

- Run a single application but keep several different documents open and available on your screen, switching from one to another whenever you want

- Run two or all three applications at the same time when you want to work on several different tasks

- Run multiple applications with multiple documents and, again, switch among them whenever you want

The only things you cannot do with Works are start the drawing module and the charting module as separate applications. As already mentioned, these programs are available only through the Word Processor and the Spreadsheet.

ONE PROGRAM, DIFFERENT GUISES

If you were to use three or more stand-alone software packages—especially non-Windows packages—to do the work that Works can do, you might sometimes feel as though you were jumping from saddle to saddle, trying to ride a number of different horses with minds of their own. Using Works, you'll feel that your software horses are pulling together as a team, and that they respond consistently and predictably to your commands.

Just because the Works applications are cooperative, though, doesn't mean that they are identical. In order to do their jobs well, the Works tools must offer you special features of their own, among them an efficient onscreen workspace designed to facilitate the type of work you want to do. When you use the Word Processor, the screen is a blank sheet onto which you can type one paragraph after the other. In the Spreadsheet, the screen resembles a page in an account book so you can organize figures and other data in rows and columns. In the Database, the same screen becomes a blank piece of drafting paper on which you can design a form for entering and organizing groups of facts.

The Word Processor

Although computers traditionally excel at crunching numbers, micro-computers are most commonly employed for crunching words instead. Figure 1-1 on the next page shows a short document as it appears in the Word Processor.

The Word Processor, more than any other part of Works, makes you feel as if you're working with a smart and very flexible typewriter. The keyboard is much the same as a typewriter keyboard, so the only real adjustment you make—at first—is getting used to seeing your words appear on the screen rather than on a piece of paper.

The great benefit of a word processor over a typewriter is that you don't have to erase or start over when you make a mistake, even when you decide to revise or reorganize a long document. You can use the screen as

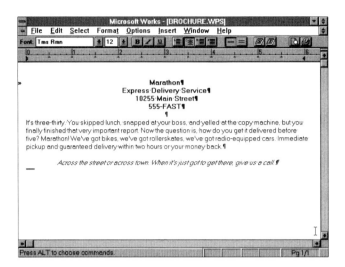

FIGURE 1-1. *The Word Processor is a powerful tool for controlling the content and appearance of your documents.*

if it were an erasable slate. You can type over words, delete paragraphs, and even move a whole section of a document by temporarily *cutting* it to a special part of memory called the Clipboard and then *pasting* it back in at a new location. You can change typefaces (*fonts*) with ease, *italicize*, **boldface**, or underline words, and change paragraph spacing and indents with a click of the mouse. Thanks to a feature called *print preview,* which is available in all the Works applications, you can even see onscreen what your document will look like when printed.

Microsoft Draw

Unlike the Word Processor, which starts at the click of a button, Microsoft Draw is a bit on the shy side. You can start it only from within a word processed document. When you reach the Draw screen, however, a world of design opens up for you. With Draw, you can create geometric patterns, drawings, monograms, and logos. If you're notorious among your friends for being unable to draw a straight line, Draw can help you out. If you need even more help, you can skip the do-it-yourself business and choose instead from a library of predrawn pictures, called *clip art,* that comes with Works. Whether you create your own graphics or rely on clip art, using Draw can help you turn an ordinary document like the one in Figure 1-1 into something like the one on the next page.

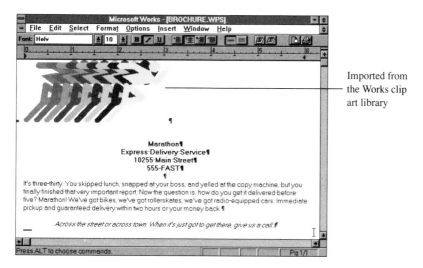

Imported from the Works clip art library

Instant visual appeal—or at least as much as your talents allow.

The Spreadsheet

When numbers, numbers are everywhere, the Spreadsheet application is the way to stay afloat. Not only can you use this Works tool as if it were an endless supply of ledger paper, you can save enormous amounts of time and trouble by letting the program do your calculating with the numbers you've typed. The following illustration shows some sample figures as you would lay them out on paper:

MYCOLA CO. - TEST MARKETING: REGULAR & RASPBERRY COLA

SALES (THOUSANDS)

REGION	REGULAR COLA		RASPBERRY COLA	
	SUGAR	DIET	SUGAR	DIET
NORTHEAST	217	57	83	49
EAST	453	498	375	369
SOUTH	322	313	231	198
MIDWEST	419	385	262	231
SOUTHWEST	153	419	137	329
NORTHWEST	347	376	362	401
TOTAL	1911	2048	1450	1577
	3959		3027	

When you work in the spreadsheet application, you can lay out the same information onscreen, as shown in the next illustration.

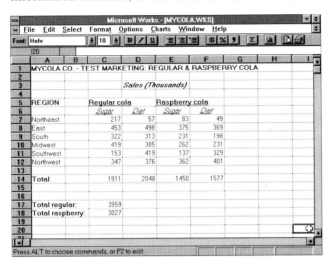

The Spreadsheet application divides your workspace into numbered rows and alphabetic columns of *cells*. Whereas typing into a word processed document feels much like typing onto a sheet of paper, typing data into a spreadsheet feels more like organizing and entering data in a columnar pad. Each cell in a spreadsheet, like the blank spaces on a ledger sheet, can contain a number (such as *83*) or some text (such as *Raspberry cola*). And the Spreadsheet is designed to let you jump easily from cell to cell and from data type to data type.

You see 20 rows and about 9 columns of cells in the illustration, but a single spreadsheet is far larger than that, as you can see for yourself by scrolling down or to the right in any spreadsheet document window. If you were patient enough to scroll to the end, you'd find that a full sheet is vast: 256 columns wide by 16,384 rows deep, for a total of 4,194,304 cells. That's more than enough for the most dedicated numbers person, especially when you consider that those 4 million cells represent a single spreadsheet and that you can create as many different spreadsheets as you have room on your disks to store them.

Charting

Numbers are strange and wonderful things, but many people—perhaps most—find pictures easier to understand. Enter charting, a quick and easy way to give visual impact to rows and columns of numbers. Starting from the Spreadsheet, you can jump into a charting program that takes a set of numbers and turns them into any of several types of charts. The following chart, for example, shows graphically how the sales volumes in the previous example compare with one another:

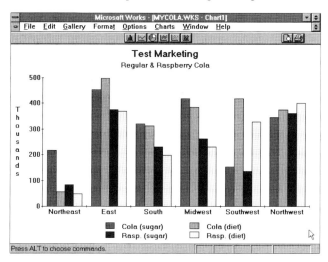

When you create a chart with Works, you can choose to print it as a separate page or you can make a copy and paste it into a word processed document. If you like, you can even *link* the chart to the pasted copy. The link is a special connection: It stays out of your way at all times, but because it exists, Works can update the copy whenever you make changes to the original—all without any additional effort on your part.

The Database

Where the word processor gives voice to your ideas and the spreadsheet makes sense of your numbers, the database application brings order to the facts that clutter and sometimes seem to clog your memory. Any group of related facts can form a *database,* and Works can help you organize and track the facts in as many databases as you want. Thus, you can create one database for names and phone numbers, another for catalog numbers, a third for parts lists, a fourth for inventories, book collections, or statistics of various types, and so on. The illustration at the top of the next page shows the types of information you would include in a database.

JELLYWORKS JELLYBEANS: CLIENT LIST

COMPANY	ADDRESS	PHONE	NOTES:
U-SAVE MARKET	12030 SE 256TH REDMOND, WA 29872	555-1010	ASK FOR CARL
GRANNY'S PANTRY	1020 S. MAIN REDMOND, WA 29872	555-2398	
KWIKSTOP	P.O. BOX 15 WOODVILLE, WA 29871	555-1234	DELIVER TO STORE ON OLD REDWAY RD.
MOSTLY KIDS	91922 378TH NW BELLMOND, WA 29869	555-4669	LOWER MALL, BE SURE TO INCLUDE BUBBLE GUM & CHOCOLATE
THE CANDY PLACE	21187 WOOD-RED RD REDMOND, WA 29872	555-4692	CLOSED WED.

The Works Database differs from the Word Processor and the Spreadsheet in one major respect: It offers you different *views* in which to work, and you can switch from one view to another with a click of the mouse button. The following illustrations show two of these views. The first, called *form view,* lets you enter information or view a single set of facts in a form you design to suit your data. Onscreen, form view looks like this:

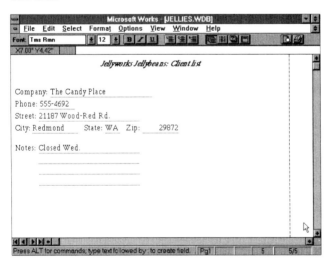

Of course, a single database can be much more extensive than the one in the example here. So when you have a large collection of records and you want to see more than one at a time, you can switch to *list view,* which looks like this:

In this example, the facts in each row correspond to the information entered on the form—a single record. However you want to work with and view your data, Works can help you do it.

Reporting

Reporting is really an integral part of the database application—more so than drawing is for the Word Processor or charting for the Spreadsheet. Reporting is simply the end result of creating and managing your data: It produces a printed copy of some or all of your records, organized in a report form you specify. The following illustration shows a report for the database in the preceding example, sorted by city, as you would see it onscreen with the Print Preview feature:

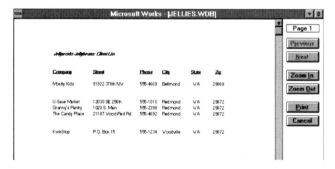

ESSENTIAL SKILLS

Now you've seen what Works is, what it can do, what it looks like, and how it varies from one application to the next. The rest of this chapter provides background information that will help you work confidently with Works, paying attention to *what* you want to do rather than *how* you're supposed to do it. These sections tell you about files, directories, menus, and dialog boxes. If you're comfortable with naming files, creating and managing directories, and using menus and dialog boxes, skip ahead to Chapter 2. If these terms are new or relatively new to you, continue on.

Disk Files

When you use any of the Works applications, you type into your computer and Works faithfully records everything you do. That's fine as far as it goes, but all your work at that point resides only in your computer's random access memory, or RAM. When work is in RAM, you can see it or print it, but when you turn your computer off, your work will disappear: RAM retains its contents only as long as your computer is provided with electricity.

To preserve your work for future use or reference, you must save it as a file on disk. Files fall into one of two basic categories: *program files,* which contain the instructions for a program such as Works, and *data files,* which contain the work you create and save. Program files are synonymous with your programs and are, or should be considered, untouchable. Data files are yours, to do with as you will.

Because you and your programs must be able to distinguish one file from another, you assign each a unique *filename.* When you're using Works, you'll be asked to provide a filename whenever you save a file for the first time. You can name a file anything you want, as long as you follow two simple rules:

1. Limit a filename to a maximum of eight characters. The name can contain any alphabetic or numeric character, but it cannot include any of the following: * + = [ ] ¦ \ : ; " < > , . ? or /.

2. Don't give *identical* filenames to two files in the same storage location, or *directory,* on a disk. (More on directories in the next section.)

A good rule of thumb to follow in assigning filenames is to make each one as descriptive as possible; meaningful names and consistent naming practices can help you recall the contents of your files later on. So, for example, if you've just created a budget for the fourth quarter, a good eight-character filename would be something like Q4BUDGET.

NOTE: *If you want, you can add a period and a three-character* extension *to a filename. You can use any of the characters valid for a filename, but avoid* *using EXE, COM, and SYS; they're reserved for program files. In using Works, you'll generally want to ignore extensions because Works automatically adds its own extensions to data files: WPS for Word Processor documents, WKS for Spreadsheet documents, and WDB for Database documents. If you stick with the Works extensions, you'll always be able to identify data files by type. In addition, Works looks for these extensions by default, so using them means you can list data files easily and completely whenever you're using Works.*

Directories

Works requires a hard disk in order to run, so it's safe to assume that you'll save most, if not all, of your files on your hard disk. A hard disk, however, can hold enormous amounts of information: anywhere from about 30 million characters, or 30 megabytes, to well over 1 billion characters, or 1 gigabyte, on some advanced designs.

Because a hard disk offers so much storage space, people tend to assume the space is endless. They also tend to forget that a computer sucks up data the way a vacuum cleaner sucks up dust. To manage all this space efficiently, you learn to rely on *directories*. Basically, a directory is a portion of disk space you name and set aside for storing related groups of files. If you want, think of files as separate packages of information and directories as containers in which you group them. Windows and Works create directories named WINDOWS and MSWORKS for themselves when they're installed on a hard disk, but you can create as many directories for data as you want or need to suit your storage purposes.

Any disk you can use for storage, hard or floppy, starts out with a single ''master'' directory called the *root,* which is always identified by a \ (backslash) character. All directories on your disk, in one way or another, eventually trace back to the root, as shown in the following illustration:

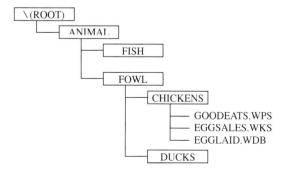

Notice that you can have directories that branch off the root directory, and you can have directories that branch off other directories. As your directory system grows, this branching effect forms a structure known as a *directory tree*.

You can't go around diagramming trees whenever you want to pinpoint a directory, so how do you refer to sub-sub-sub-branches of a directory tree or to the files they contain? You write out their locations as a *path*. A path normally begins with the root directory and includes the entire string of directories, separated by backslashes, to a particular directory or file. For example, you would write out the path to the data file GOODEATS.WPS in the preceding example like this:

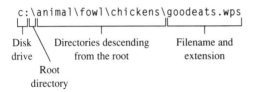

You encounter paths and directories in your work with Works whenever you open and save files. The following illustration shows both a path and a list of directories as they appear in a Works dialog box:

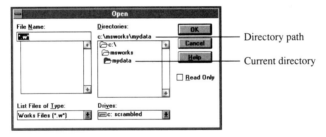

Just below the portion of this dialog box headed *Directories* you can see the directory path *c:\msworks\mydata*. In the box below the path, you see the same path displayed graphically. Notice that each directory level in the path is shown separately, and that successive levels below the root are indented farther and farther to the right. The dark highlight on *mydata* tells you that it is the *current directory*, the one Works will use in searching for or saving files.

When directories are listed in a dialog box, you can change from one to another by double-clicking on the name of the directory you want. If a directory is on the same disk but not in the current path, double-click on the root (*c:*) to see a list of all directories that branch from there.

Creating a directory

To create a directory, you can use either Windows or MS-DOS. If you use Windows, the process is as follows:

1. Using the Program Manager, find the File Manager icon in the group window titled Main.
2. Double-click on the icon to start the File Manager.
3. Click on the directory in which you want to create the new directory.
4. Click on the File menu to open it.
5. Click on the Create Directory command.

When you choose Create Directory, Windows displays a dialog box like this one:

Type *mydata* to create the directory C:\MSWORKS\MYDATA.

Check the current directory Windows displays at the top of the dialog box. If you want to create a directory under the current directory, simply type its name. If you want to create a directory in a different part of your directory tree, click Cancel, highlight the directory you want, and then choose Create Directory again.

To create a directory from the MS-DOS prompt, use the Make Directory command, abbreviating it as *md*. Type the new directory name as described above for the Windows dialog box.

Directory Assistance

Directories are an important concept for managing your Works files — one with which many MS-DOS and Windows users are already quite comfortable. If you need more information on directories, see

■ Your Windows manual

■ Any book on MS-DOS that deals with directories

■ Any book on Windows that deals with the File Manager

MENUS AND DIALOG BOXES

Much of your activity with Works will involve giving *commands* that tell Works what to do next. Because some commands are used far more often than others, Works offers you the Toolbar as a quick, "click-and-run" alternative to menu choices. Often, however, you'll rely on menus to carry out commands that aren't accessible through the Toolbar.

Using menus is easy: All you have to do is learn roughly what each menu contains and then choose what you want. To use a menu,

1. Point to the menu name and click the left mouse button, or press Alt and the underlined letter in the menu name. Either of these actions *opens* the menu.

2. Point to the command you want to use and click again, or press the underlined letter in the command you want. Either of these actions *chooses* the command.

Sometimes choosing a command causes Works to act immediately. At other times, however, choosing a command causes Works to display a dialog box. At still other times, choosing a command can do nothing at all. How can you tell what will happen? The next illustration explains these differences; it also shows how you can tell whether Works offers a *keyboard shortcut* you can use instead of going through the menu:

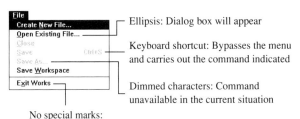

Ellipsis: Dialog box will appear

Keyboard shortcut: Bypasses the menu and carries out the command indicated

Dimmed characters: Command unavailable in the current situation

No special marks:
Command carried out immediately

Sometimes you'll notice that a command that was dimmed (and thus not available) the last time you opened a menu appears in dark characters the next time you use the same menu. Don't be surprised. Works turns commands on and off automatically to suit the situation. In a similar fashion, it sometimes changes the wording of a command to provide you with a more helpful description. Be grateful—it's all part of the service.

Dialog Boxes

As you can tell from its name, a dialog box is the means that voiceless Works uses to hold a conversation with you. In real life, a conversation can be brief and to the point, or it can be longer and more detailed. The same is true of dialog boxes.

At its simplest, a dialog box can be as easy to use as the Startup dialog box, in which you do nothing more than click the button of your choice. Typically, however, a dialog box relies on one or more special elements to ask for your choices or for needed information. The following list, with its accompanying illustrations, identifies these elements:

■ A *text box* is a rectangular box into which you type some information Works cannot guess at—for example, a name for a file you want to save. You can type into a text box whenever a blinking vertical bar, the *insertion point,* is in it.

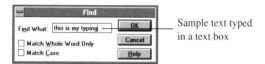

Sample text typed in a text box

■ A *list box* is similar to a text box, but instead of typing into it, you choose from a list of valid possibilities. A list box can contain a vertical scroll bar. To make a choice, scroll if necessary and then click on the item you want. In some cases, the list is hidden from view until you click on a downward-pointing arrow at the right edge.

List box with scroll bar

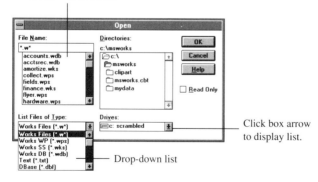

Click box arrow to display list.

Drop-down list

■ In addition to list boxes and text boxes, dialog boxes can also contain *check boxes* and *option buttons*. A check box is a small, square box to the left of an option; you can turn the item on or off by clicking in the box. An option button is a small round "button." Click the button to turn it on; to turn it off, select a different option button.

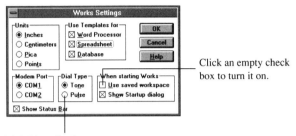

Click an empty check box to turn it on.

Click this option button to turn on Pulse and turn off Tone.

If an item with a check box is turned on, an X appears in the box; if an item with an option button is turned on, the button contains a dark circle. Notice that the section titled *Use Templates For* has all three of its check boxes turned on, but none of the sections containing option buttons has more than one turned on. When you see a group of check boxes, you can turn on as many as you need; when you see a set of option buttons, you can choose only one at a time.

■ Finally, all dialog boxes contain *command buttons* that you click just as you do the buttons in the Startup dialog box. Typically, dialog boxes contain three buttons labeled *OK*, *Cancel*, and *Help*:

Click to close the box and put into effect any choices you made.

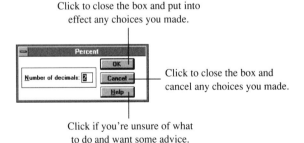

Click to close the box and cancel any choices you made.

Click if you're unsure of what to do and want some advice.

That's it. You've covered the essential background information you need to use Works confidently. The remainder of the book turns you loose with Works.

CHAPTER 2

Starting, Stopping, and Using Files

Whenever you use Works, you type data into a *document.* As you work, you use the mouse or the keyboard to move from place to place in the document. Because Works lets you keep several different documents on the screen at the same time, you can also use the mouse or keyboard to move from one task to another.

When you finish working with a document, you save it as a *file* on disk and *close* the file. When you finish using Works, you clean up and shut down by saving any document changes you want to keep and then *exiting* the program. This chapter describes the different ways you can start and stop Works, as well as ways to open, close, and save your files. The topics covered include the following:

■ Starting Works

■ Opening a new file

■ Opening a previously saved file

■ Closing a file

■ Starting a WorksWizard

■ Saving your work

■ Stopping Works

■ Saving your workspace so you can pick up where you left off

■ Tailoring Works to your preferences

■ Using Templates and Sample Documents

STARTING WORKS

The introductory chapter described how to start Works from the Windows Program Manager. On many computers, you can also start Works directly from the MS-DOS prompt. If Works does not appear automatically whenever you start your computer, your two basic startup options are as follows:

■ From the Windows Program Manager, double-click on the Works icon in the SolutionSeries window. You'll most likely use this option all or almost all the time. (If you can't see the SolutionSeries window or the Works icon, refer to the section "What Happens If..." in the introduction.)

■ From the MS-DOS prompt (C:\>), enter the command

```
cd \msworks
```

to tell MS-DOS to change to the Works program directory.
Next, type

```
msworks
```

and press Enter. The second command starts Works, and, because Works needs Windows, it starts Windows as well.

OPENING FILES

Whenever you use Works, you can open and close document files at will. You can open a new file, or *create* a file, even if you're already working on another.

To open a new file at startup or at any time during a Works session,

■ If the Startup dialog box is onscreen, click the button for the application you want. Doing this both starts the application and opens a new file in which you can begin to create a new document.

■ If the Startup dialog box is not onscreen, choose Create New File from the File menu. Doing this displays a dialog box similar to the Startup dialog:

Click the button for the application in which you want to create the file. The application will start with a blank screen for the new document.

To open a previously saved file at startup or during a Works session,

■ If the Startup dialog box is onscreen, click the Open Existing File button.

■ If the Startup dialog box is not onscreen, open the File menu and choose the Open Existing File command.

Whether you choose Open Existing File at startup or while you're using Works, the dialog box shown in Figure 2-1 appears. If the name of the file you want isn't displayed, type the filename (including drive and path if appropriate) in the File Name box. Or use the following techniques to search for the file:

■ If the file is on a different disk, click the arrow in the Drives box. When Works displays a list of disk drives, click the one you want.

■ If the file is in a different directory, double-click directory names in the Directories box to move through your directory tree to the one you want. As you select different directories, Works updates the File Name box to reflect your choice.

■ Normally, Works displays filenames of all Works document files (for the selected drive and directory). If you want to see files of a particular type, click the arrow in the List Files of Type box. When Works displays a list of file types, click the type you want. For example, choose *Works WP* to see only Works word processing files (those with the filename extension WPS). Any matching filenames in your

The list of filenames changes as you select different drives, directories, and document types.

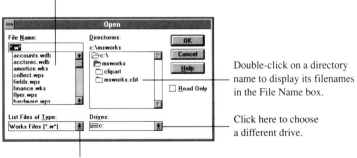

Double-click on a directory name to display its filenames in the File Name box.

Click here to choose a different drive.

Click here to choose a different type of file to display in the File Name box.

FIGURE 2-1. *To find the file you want to open, you sometimes need to choose a different drive, directory, or file type.*

chosen drive and directory will then appear in the File Name box. Notice that some choices, such as *DBase* and *WordPerfect 5.1*, allow you to open files created with programs other than Works.

To open one of the last four files you used, Works offers a quick alternative to the Open Existing File command:

1. If the Startup dialog box is onscreen, click the Cancel button. (Skip this step if you're already in a Works session.)

2. Open the File menu. At the bottom of the menu, Works displays the names of the last four files you used. Click the file's name to open the file and start the appropriate application.

STARTING A WORKSWIZARD

In keeping with its ease-of-use philosophy, Works includes several "prerecorded" sets of commands that appear as colorful, graphic tools that help you through the process of creating an address book, a form letter, or a set of mailing labels. These tools, the WorksWizards, are accessible either through the Startup dialog box or from the Create New File command. To use them

- If the Startup dialog box is onscreen, click the WorksWizards button.

- If the Startup dialog box is not onscreen, choose the Create New File command and click the WorksWizards button in the dialog box that appears.

When you request the WorksWizards, Works responds with a dialog box that asks you to choose the kind of document you want to create:

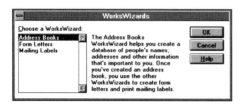

- If you know which WorksWizard you want, double-click on its name to start it.

- Alternatively, click (just once) on the name of a WorksWizard, both to choose it and to see (in the middle of the dialog box) a description of what it does. Click OK to start.

NOTE: *Even though you have a choice of WorksWizards, the three are not totally independent. The Form Letters and Mailing Labels WorksWizards both rely on a previously prepared mailing list, and the Form Letters WorksWizard also needs an existing letter it can customize for you. You can prepare a mailing list either on your own or with the Address Books WorksWizard. The letter for the Form Letters WorksWizard is easy to prepare with the word processor. Chapter 10 tells you more about form letters and mailing lists.*

When you start a WorksWizard, you see an opening screen like the one in Figure 2-2. The WorksWizards are remarkably easy to use. Instructions abound, and because each WorksWizard follows a predetermined set of commands from beginning to end, you can trust it to prompt you through the entire process of creating whatever type of file it's designed to create.

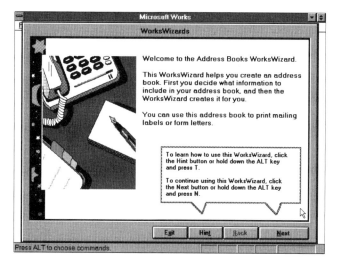

FIGURE 2-2. *The initial screen for the Address Books WorksWizard.*

For the most part, the WorksWizards go through the give and take of finding out what you want by displaying sets of options and asking you to make choices. Because the WorksWizards are so carefully constructed, you're unlikely to need help in using them. If you become uncertain or change your mind, however,

■ Click the Hint button for advice on using the WorksWizard.

■ Click the Back button as many times as necessary to back up through previous steps. When you reach the step you want, make whatever changes you feel are needed.

■ Click the Exit button if you want to escape the procedure.

Even if you do make mistakes, by the way, there's no real harm done. You simply end up with an incorrectly designed address book, form letter, or mailing-label file on disk. At worst, you'll mutter insults to yourself as you rerun the WorksWizard.

NOTE: *To avoid cluttering your hard disk or later confusing the good file with the bad one, be sure to delete the imperfect file before you forget what it is and what you named it. You can't delete files while you're within Works, so use either the Delete command on the Windows File Manager's File menu or use the MS-DOS Del command.*

CLOSING A FILE

Whenever you finish using a file and want to put it away, you use the Close command on the File menu. If you've saved all changes to the document before you choose the Close command, Works packs the file away and removes its onscreen window. If the file contains any unsaved changes, however, Works displays the dialog box shown in Figure 2-3, asking if you want to save the changes:

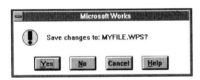

FIGURE 2-3. *Works will always ask if you want to save your changes before it closes a file.*

- Click Yes to save the file. If the file has already been named, Works saves the changes and then closes the file. If the file has never before been saved, Works takes you to the Save As command described below so that you can provide a filename. After you name the file, Works carries out the Close command.

- Click No to toss away your changes. Choosing the Close command and clicking No is a good way to keep your disk uncluttered: If you have not yet saved a document and you really don't want to keep it, just say no.

- Click Cancel to cancel the Close command and keep the file open.

- Click Help for advice on what to do.

SAVING YOUR WORK

When you work with a computer, you must either save your work on disk or lose your work when you exit the program or turn off the machine. As you work, you should save periodically (and often!) as a precaution against losing any work in progress—in the event a software, hardware, or electrical problem puts an abrupt end to your computing session. In addition to saving periodically, save your open, changed documents at the end of a session if you want to keep all the work you've done.

Save and Save As

Whether you're saving a document during a work session or prior to ending the session and quitting Works, you use either of two commands on the File menu, Save or Save As:

■ Save stores a file on disk, under its current name and in the current directory of the disk in the current drive. Save doesn't ask for a drive, directory, or filename, so use it to save an already named file.

■ Save As also stores a file on disk, but it first produces a dialog box asking you to name the file. Use this command to save a newly created file or one that you want to rename, save in a different directory, or save on a different disk.

NOTE: *Works gives every new document a temporary name (WORD1, WORD2, SHEET1, SHEET2, DATA1, DATA2, and so on), but you can't use Save to save documents under these names. If you try to use Save, Works assumes you made a mistake and gives you the Save As command.*

Works carries out the Save command immediately. When you choose Save As, however, Works displays this dialog box:

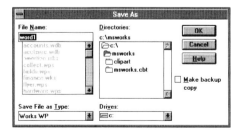

To save the file,

1. Type a filename. To delete characters displayed in the box, click just in front of or behind them and drag the highlight over the characters

you want to replace. Your subsequent typing will replace the high-lighted characters.

2. If necessary, move on to the other boxes (Directories, Save File As Type, and Drives) to specify the storage location of your choice.

3. Check the option Make Backup Copy if you want Works to make a copy of the file as it was before you started working on it. Works makes (or updates) a backup copy of the file each time you save, until you click on the check box again to clear it.

Using Backups

Backup copies can come in handy. For example, you might edit your working copy of a document beyond redemption and want to start over with the earlier version *after* you have already saved the changes. If you need the backup, choose the Open Existing File command and click on All Files in the List Files Of Type box. Works displays the names of all files in the specified directory. Your backup copy has the same filename as your original file, but the backup will have a different extension—BPS, BKS, or BDB—as shown in the following table:

File type	Original	Backup
Word processor	topnotch.wps	topnotch.bps
Spreadsheet	moolah.wks	moolah.bks
Database	biglist.wdb	biglist.bdb

To rename the backup copy as a regular Works file, open it, use the Save As command, and either type the normal extension or choose the appropriate file type in the Save File as Type box.

SAVING YOUR WORKSPACE

If you're in the middle of a project when you decide to close up shop for awhile, you don't have to pack all your work away, only to spend time re-creating the same arrangement of open files—the same *workspace*—the next time you start Works. You can leave all the remembering to Works with the Save Workspace command on the File menu.

Saving your workspace is useful whether you're working on one document or many. When you save your workspace, you essentially tell Works to take a snapshot of the screen. The next time you start Works, it consults that snapshot to rebuild your workspace exactly.

To save your workspace,

1. Save any newly created documents that you want to preserve as part of your workspace.

2. Choose Save Workspace from the File menu. If the workspace includes some new, unsaved documents, you see the following message:

If you see this message, you can do one of three things: Click Cancel and then save any files you want to preserve as part of your workspace, click OK if you don't want to save any other files as part of the workspace, or click Help if you want advice on what to do.

After you choose Save Workspace, your disk drive becomes active for a short time, and you see the message *Saving Workspace: xx% Completed* in the status bar at the bottom of the screen. When saving is complete, you can exit Works knowing that you'll be able to start up again where you left off.

When you choose the Save Workspace command, notice that Works turns on the Use Saved Workspace option in the Works Settings dialog box (shown in Figure 2-4 on page 27). As long as that option is turned on, Works will continue to load your saved workspace when you start the program. Bear in mind, however, that your "saved workspace" refers to the condition of your screen as it was when you last used the Save Workspace command, not as it was when you last exited Works. If you open or close documents after using the Save Workspace command, Works does not update its record of your workspace simply because the Use Saved Workspace option is turned on. You must reuse the Save Workspace command if you want to update the record.

STOPPING WORKS

The complement of starting a program is, obviously, stopping it. What might not be so obvious, however, is that you must explicitly tell a program to put itself away. In particular, stopping a program is not the same as turning off your computer. When you stop a program, or exit, you give it a chance to put away your files and ensure that all the work you want to save is neatly and accessibly stored on disk. Turning off your computer while a program is running means that you lose all the work you haven't saved and that you run the risk of damaging your hard disk. Stopping a program by flipping the power switch is like stopping a bicycle by running into a tree: It works, but is it smart?

The proper way to stop Works is to,

1. Save all open files that contain unsaved changes.

2. Use the Save Workspace command if you find it advantageous.

3. Choose the Exit Works command on the File menu.

Although saving before quitting should become a habit with you, don't worry if, on occasion, you forget to save a file. Works has a built-in resistance to leaving any unfinished business when it quits, so if it detects any unsaved work as it prepares to shut down, it tells you so with the dialog box you saw in Figure 2-3. If you have more than one open file with unsaved changes, Works displays the same dialog box for each before it finally exits and returns you to Windows.

CUSTOMIZING WORKS

The preceding section on saving your workspace mentioned the Use Saved Workspace option in the Works Settings dialog box. This box includes a number of other options as well, all of which enable you to customize Works to your needs and preferences.

To adjust any settings, choose the Works Settings command from the Option menu. When you choose the command, the dialog box shown in Figure 2-4 appears.

The following list describes each of the option categories. If you need more information, click the Help button in the dialog box.

- Units: Lets you specify the unit of measure you want to use for page margins and other such settings. The choices are inches, centimeters, picas (⅙ inch), and points (a printer's measure, roughly ¹⁄₇₂ inch). Even though you choose a setting here, you're also free to use any other unit of measure whenever you want. For example, if you use Inches as the Units setting, you can still specify a margin as *2.54 cm*, *6 pi* (picas), or *72 pt* (points). Works will convert the measurement to your standard unit automatically.

- Modem Port: Lets you tell Works which port, or connector, your modem (if any) is attached to. COM1 is typical, but if your computer

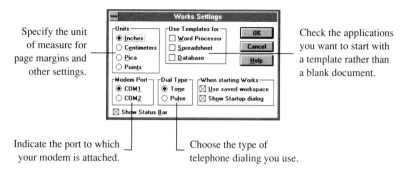

Specify the unit of measure for page margins and other settings.

Check the applications you want to start with a template rather than a blank document.

Indicate the port to which your modem is attached.

Choose the type of telephone dialing you use.

FIGURE 2-4. *You can customize Works in the Works Settings dialog box.*

has more than one serial (communications) port, your modem connection might be different. If you have a modem, Works can use it with the Dial This Number command on the Options menu to phone a number you highlight in a document. Making this type of connection enables you to establish voice, not computer-to-computer, communication.

■ Dial Type: Lets you indicate the type of dialing your telephone uses, tone or rotary.

■ Use Templates For: Lets you tailor Works to start the application you specify by opening a template instead of a blank document. A template is a document model in which you design and save the layout, formatting, and even standard text for a particular type of document that you routinely create with the application. The next section, "Using Templates and Sample Documents," tells more about setting up and using templates.

■ When Starting Works: Lets you customize the way you start Works. Turn on Use Saved Workspace to return to your previous work at startup. Turn off Show Startup Dialog if you want to skip the Startup dialog box and start Works with a blank application workspace.

■ Show Status Bar: Turns on or off the status bar at the bottom of the screen. Turn off the status bar if you want to gain an extra line of screen space.

USING TEMPLATES AND SAMPLE DOCUMENTS

Works offers you two ways to speed up your work: the templates briefly mentioned in the preceding section, and a set of sample documents that come with the Works program.

Templates

Templates are "boilerplate" document forms that you design and save for use in creating a particular type of document, such as a business letter or a budget spreadsheet. To create a workable template, you must be able to use the application that the template is intended for, but unless you need a complex layout, you shouldn't have much trouble. In fact, the best way to create a template is to experiment with the design, layout, and contents of a document you know you'll use a great deal. Once you're satisfied with the design of a prospective template, strip out any unnecessary text or graphics so that you have the basic framework you need the next time you create the same kind of document. At that point, you can save the document as a template and avoid having to repeat the same experimentation you just went through. Your template needn't be absolutely perfect, either, because you can always modify and fine-tune it later on and save it again.

Later chapters in this book describe features of the Word Processor, Spreadsheet, and Database that you might need in creating a template. Figure 2-5 shows a sample budget spreadsheet that you could save as a template.

Once you've created a template, here's how to save what you've done:

1. Choose the Save As command from the File menu.
2. Click on the downward-pointing arrow at the right of the Save File As Type box.
3. Choose the template option. For example, in the Spreadsheet choose *SS Template.*
4. Click OK.

Now, whenever you create a new file with that application, you'll see the template you designed. You can customize the document any way you want. When you save the result, Works stores it as a normal Works document, thus keeping your template uncluttered.

If you do not want to use the template every time you start the related Works application, take the following steps:

1. Choose the Works Settings command from the Options menu.
2. Click in the Use Templates For section of the Settings dialog box to turn off the check box for the type of template you created.

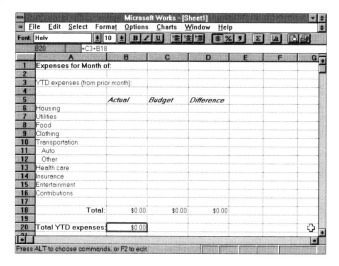

FIGURE 2-5. *A sample Spreadsheet template.*

If you decide to save a document as a template, bear in mind that Works saves only one template per application. You cannot, for example, create a Spreadsheet template for tracking manufacturing costs and another for tracking sales.

With a little discipline, however, you can have more than a single template for an application, but you'll have to save your auxiliary templates as normal document files. When you want to use one of your "templates," open the file and enter whatever data you want, and then be sure to save the modified document under a new name. Your template document will remain on disk, under its old name, where you can return to it whenever you want. Treating normal files as templates in this way is useful if you create a certain type of document often.

Sample Documents

If you choose the Open Existing File command on the File menu and look at the list of files in the MSWORKS directory, you see a list of files with names such as ACCOUNTS.WDB, ACCTSREC.WDB, FINANCE.WKS, and FLYER.WPS. These are the names of sample documents that Microsoft ships with Works. You can open, view, and change any of these documents. They are particularly useful for

■ Serving as the basis for a document of the same type that you want to create

■ Seeing how the Works developers themselves decided to organize and lay out such a document

Figure 2-6 shows part of the accounts receivable sample document.

Notice that instructions are included in boldfaced italics wherever necessary and that a block of text in the lower right corner tells you how to make changes to the form. Given these instructions, plus a little knowledge of the application itself, you can put these sample documents to work on your own data in short order.

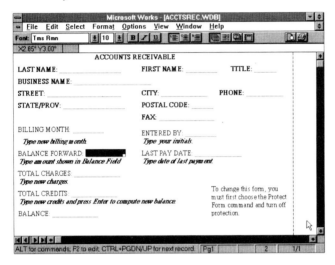

FIGURE 2-6. *The accounts receivable sample document, ACCTSREC.WBD.*

If you modify one of the sample documents but want to keep the original for reference or as a clean resource in case your changes don't quite do the job, save your version with a different filename, preferably in a directory other than MSWORKS.

Chapter 3

Managing Windows and Getting Help

As a Windows program, Works gives you considerable control over the shape, size, and arrangement of both your application and document windows. In addition, it displays a constant but unobtrusive stream of messages in the status bar at the bottom of your screen. All the while, the Help menu stands ready: Through it, Works offers a wealth of Windows-style Help information—tailored to your situation and easy to navigate.

This chapter tells you how to customize open windows on your screen and how to get help. Topics include

- Maximizing and minimizing windows
- Changing window sizes
- Arranging multiple windows onscreen
- Splitting windows
- Using Help

MANAGING WINDOWS

To get around in Works, you need to learn two types of mobility: moving within a single document and moving among several open documents. Later chapters tell you about the many ways you can navigate within a document. In this section, you'll see the bigger picture. You'll learn how to size and arrange multiple onscreen windows so you can move among them easily, and you'll learn how to split single windows so that you can see different parts of the same document.

Maximizing and Minimizing Windows

Works, like Windows, always displays a *maximize* button and a *minimize* button in the upper right corner of the application window. In addition, Works displays both buttons in the same place in every document window you open. What this means to you is that you can expand and shrink either the entire Works application window or any of the individual document windows:

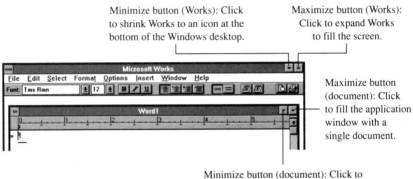

Minimize button (Works): Click to shrink Works to an icon at the bottom of the Windows desktop.

Maximize button (Works): Click to expand Works to fill the screen.

Maximize button (document): Click to fill the application window with a single document.

Minimize button (document): Click to shrink a document to an icon at the bottom of the Works application window.

Clicking any of these buttons gives you the following advantages:

- Maximizing the application window expands Works to take full advantage of your onscreen work area. When Works fills the screen, the maximize button changes to a *restore* button with two arrowheads, one pointing up and the other down. Click the restore button to return the application window to its former size.

- Minimizing the application window temporarily gives the screen back to Windows. Works and your documents remain active, but they're in "suspended animation"; minimizing Works is ideal when you want to use another Windows application for awhile.

- Maximizing a document window gives a single document as much room as possible onscreen. When you maximize a document window, its minimize button disappears, and any other open windows are covered up. You can return to them, however, either by clicking the document window's restore button or by choosing the document you want from the list of open windows that Works displays at the bottom of the Window menu.

- Minimizing a document window moves it out of your way without closing the file. When you want to display several documents side by side, as described later, you can conserve screen space by minimizing the documents that you rarely need.

Changing Window Sizes

Useful as they are, maximizing and minimizing are essentially "all or nothing" choices. For the times you need something in between, Works, like Windows, offers movable window borders. Unless the window (application or document) has been maximized, you can use the mouse to resize it, by dragging the border or corner:

- Dragging a horizontal or vertical *border* toward the edge of the screen expands the window in the direction you drag. Dragging a border toward the center of the window shrinks the window in the same direction.

- Dragging a window *corner* toward the edge of the screen lets you pull both the horizontal and vertical borders outward at the same time, expanding the window in both directions. Dragging a corner toward the center of the window has the reverse effect.

When the mouse is in position to resize a window, its onscreen pointer changes from a single-headed arrow to a double-headed arrow:

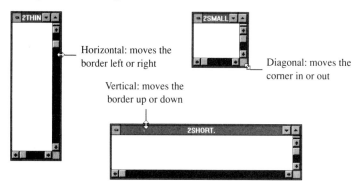

Horizontal: moves the border left or right

Vertical: moves the border up or down

Diagonal: moves the corner in or out

Arranging Multiple Windows Onscreen

Works allows you to open as many as eight separate documents, displaying each in its own window. You'll especially appreciate this capability as you take greater advantage of Works capabilities—by copying, moving, and combining data from multiple documents created with more than one application.

To open multiple windows, use the Create New File or the Open Existing File command for each document you want to create or use. Once you've opened these documents, you can arrange them by

- Cascading the windows in an overlapping pattern, like shingles on a roof
- Tiling the windows—placing them side by side, like tiles in a mosaic
- Minimizing one or more windows as icons along the bottom of the application window

Cascading and tiling windows

Works normally cascades multiple onscreen windows, placing the active window—the one containing the document you're working with—on top of the pile. Cascaded windows have the advantage of devoting the majority (but not all) of the screen space to the document that's currently occupying your attention. Cascading, however, covers up your other open documents. To display at least a portion of each open document, tile the windows, thereby giving each a piece of the screen. You can switch back and forth between cascaded and tiled windows whenever you want by choosing Cascade or Tile from the Window menu.

Moving among windows

Whether windows are cascaded or tiled, you can move from one document to another in several ways:

- By clicking in the window you want. This is the easiest method if windows are tiled or if enough of an overlapped window is visible for you to be sure it's the one you want.
- By opening the Window menu and choosing the document by name from the list of open documents. This method works well when you have a lot of cascaded windows and cannot determine from the exposed portions which is which.
- By using two keyboard shortcuts: Ctrl-F6 to move forward to the next document window in the "chain," and Ctrl-Shift-F6 (produced by pressing all three keys at the same time) to move backward to the previous document window. This method is handy if you're especially comfortable using a keyboard.

Minimizing windows

If you've opened a number of document windows but use some of them far more than others, you can minimize the less important documents;

as icons, they'll be out of the way but still accessible. You minimize a document window just as you do an application window: by clicking the minimize button at the upper right corner of the window.

When Works minimizes document windows, it lines them up from left to right along the bottom of the application window. If one or more document windows extend all the way to the bottom of the application window, however, a minimized document can seem to disappear. Don't panic; it's still there. To make its icon visible, choose either the Cascade or Tile command from the Window menu. Either command tells Works to rearrange the screen, after which the icon will appear at the bottom of the window. To restore a document icon, double-click on it.

Splitting Windows

In addition to arranging whole windows, you can also split a document window by dividing it into panes separated by a split bar. Inside the panes you can display different parts of a single document—to see the beginning and end of a long report, for example, or to compare columns of figures in a spreadsheet. Figure 3-1 on the next page shows a split window in the Works Word Processor.

In the Word Processor, you can split a window into upper and lower panes and scroll independently in each. In the Spreadsheet, and in the spreadsheetlike Database format called list view, you can split a window horizontally and vertically into four panes. When you produce such a four-way split, pairs of windows scroll "in synch" so that you don't lose track of where you are by wandering in different directions to the far corners of your document. Thus, in a window split four ways:

- The two lefthand panes and the two righthand panes scroll horizontally in unison so that they scan across the same relative regions of your document.

- The top two panes and the bottom two panes scroll vertically in unison so that they, too, show the same relative regions of your document.

To split a window, you can either choose the Split command on the Window menu or drag a small, rectangular split box to the place where you want the division to occur.

The Split command

When you choose the Split command, Works displays a gray horizontal bar (in the Word Processor) or a pair of intersecting vertical and

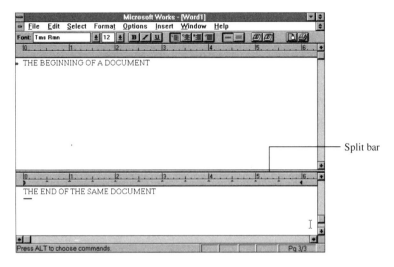

FIGURE 3-1. *Splitting a document window can let you view widely separated parts of a document.*

horizontal bars (in the Spreadsheet and Database). Arrowheads in the center of the bars show how you can adjust their position:

1. Use the arrow keys or move the mouse to move the bar (or bars) to the location at which you want to split the window.

2. Press Enter or click the mouse button to create the split (or splits).

The split boxes

The split boxes in the scroll bars respond only to the mouse. Split boxes appear at the top of the vertical scroll bar in all three Works applications and at the far left edge of the horizontal scroll bar in the Spreadsheet and Database. When the mouse pointer is in position on a split box, it looks like this:

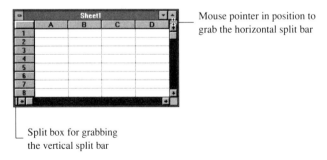

To split the window, drag the split box to the place at which you want the window divided. Release the mouse button to create the split. To quickly split a window in half, double-click on the split box.

Traversing panes and removing splits

You can move among the panes of a document using either the mouse or the keyboard:

- Click with the mouse in the pane you want.

- Press F6 to move clockwise or Shift-F6 to move counterclockwise.

To restore a split window to a single pane, whether you've used the Split command or the split boxes, do one of the following:

- Double-click on the split bar separating the panes.

- Drag the split bar to the edge of the window.

- Choose the Split command and use the arrow keys to move the split bar to the edge of the window.

GETTING HELP

When you request help, Works displays part of a detailed, disk-based "manual" to which you can refer any time you want. This feature, called online Help, is indexed in such a way that you can pick and choose the topics you want to read about. Click on a topic, and Works jumps to it, no matter where you started or where you want to go. You can request Help in any of three ways:

- With the Help button in a dialog box

- With the Help menu that appears in the menu bar, no matter which application you're using

- By pressing the F1 key (in most circumstances)

When you request Help, Works opens a window similar to the one you see with Windows Help:

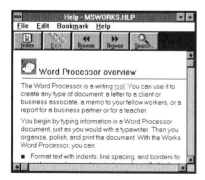

Help offers you several ways to find and request aid with a specific command or procedure. The information is extensively cross-referenced and easy to browse:

- Click on any topic marked with a solid underline to move to that topic.

- Click on the vertical scroll bar (a horizontal bar might be displayed but is inactive) to move through a topic longer than one windowful.

- Point to any term marked with a dotted underline, and then press *and hold* the mouse button to see a definition of the term. (If you have version 3.1 of Windows, simply click the mouse button to see a definition. Click again to close the definition.)

Beyond these techniques, the following brief descriptions should be enough to help you navigate into and through online Help.

The Help Menu

The Help menu gives you access to several broad Help categories. From the menu, choose one of the following commands:

- Overview to request a general introduction to Works or any of its applications except Draw. If you haven't opened a menu or chosen a command, you can request an overview by pressing the F1 key.

- Index to request a list of available Help topics. Every underlined entry in the list represents a topic you can choose by clicking on it. To avoid presenting you with a long, unwieldy list of topics and subtopics, the Index begins with a few broad topics. From that point, you choose from successively more detailed lists until you (usually) find the information you seek.

- Basic Skills to read up on Works basics, such as working with windows and documents. Use this if you're feeling confused or need to jog your memory about Works in general, as opposed to one of its applications or commands.

- Keyboard Shortcuts for information about using the keyboard instead of the mouse. Because this Help topic describes many keystrokes and key combinations that let you use Works efficiently, you'll find the topic useful whether or not you have a mouse.

- How To Use Help if you need assistance with Help. The information you see isn't very detailed, but once the Help window opens, you can get all the help you want by pressing the F1 key. Within Help, F1 takes you to an index to using Help that's both thorough and good.

■ Tutorial to start a special set of interactive lessons that teach you how to use Works. (See Figure 3-2.) The tutorial is divided into six major topics ranging from *Starting with Computers* through *Using Tools Together*. You can pick and choose lessons and work at your own pace. The lessons are short, well-designed, and easy to absorb, and the tutorial is useful for anyone who wants to learn about Works— newcomers and old hands alike.

FIGURE 3-2. *The Tutorial offers lessons on six major topics.*

■ The final item on the Help menu, About Microsoft Works, is not a "real" Help topic. Choosing this item produces a dialog box that gives copyright and licensing information about your copy of Works.

The Help Window

Although you might expect the Help window to be a small, TV-like region of the screen on which Works displays advice, it's actually quite a bit more. Help is an application in its own right, and its menus and buttons give you a great deal of latitude in using Help. At the top of the window, in their usual locations, are the control menu and the maximize and minimize buttons.

The minimize button is useful if you want to shrink the window to an icon and yet keep Help close at hand. When you minimize the Help window, however, don't be surprised if it seems to disappear, especially if your Works application window is maximized. The Help icon, unlike document icons, *doesn't* appear at the bottom of the Works window. It appears, instead, at the bottom of your Windows desktop. To use Help when it's minimized, do one of the following:

■ Minimize the Works window temporarily so you can see the Help icon.

■ Shorten the Works window so that the bottom of the Windows desktop and at least part of the Help icon are visible.

The Help menus

The Help window offers four menus:

■ File enables you to print a Help topic, set up your printer, or exit Help. The menu also includes an Open (file) option you can use to view Help for other Windows programs that you've installed, such as Microsoft Publisher, the desktop publishing program in the Solution Series. You're unlikely to need this option.

■ Edit lets you copy a Help topic to the Clipboard or add your own annotations—notes of your own—to a topic. When you copy Help to the Clipboard, you can then insert the information into a document, such as a printed ''manual'' of your own. When you annotate a Help topic, Works displays a small paper clip at the beginning of the topic. Clicking on the paper clip displays your note.

■ Bookmark lets you insert text that acts as a bookmark—your onscreen equivalent of a sticky tag or scrap of paper for marking a selected ''page'' (topic) in Help. When you create a bookmark, Help proposes the topic heading as the bookmark name, but you can type a more descriptive name of your choosing. After you create a bookmark, Help displays its name at the bottom of the Bookmark menu. To jump to the bookmark, simply click on its name.

■ Help takes you to information on using Help. For speed, press the F1 key instead of choosing from the menu.

The Help buttons

Below the Help menus is a set of Help buttons, all dedicated to helping you move through Help topics effortlessly. This is what the buttons do:

 Index displays the Help index. Click this button whenever you want to return to the Index from a Help topic.

 Back takes you to the previous Help topic you viewed. If the button is dimmed, there is no previous topic to return to.

Browse (back) and Browse (forward) let you move sequentially through topics and subtopics. The Browse buttons are useful when you want to scan the contents of Help for particular information.

 Search opens a dialog box (shown below) in which you can specify a subject you want to find. Help will display any topics dealing with that subject in the lower list box. Highlight the topic you want and click Go To; Help will move directly to that topic.

Scroll through the list of subjects or type the first few letters of a subject to which you want to jump.

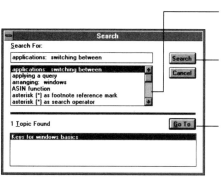

Click the Search button to display related topics in the lower box.

Click here to display information on the highlighted topic (in the lower box).

CHAPTER 4

Word Processing Basics

Turn to the Word Processor whenever you want to share your thoughts with the world. Of all the Works applications, the Word Processor is the one most likely to feel "natural"—similar as it is in use to the typewriter it replaces. Even so, there's more to processing words than typing. This chapter tells you how to

- Create and edit a document
- Check spelling and find synonyms
- Format a document to make it look good
- Check page breaks and preview a document
- Print a document

GETTING STARTED

As described in Chapter 2, you can start the Word Processor in one of two ways:

- Click the Word Processor button in either the Startup dialog box or the Create New File dialog box.
- Choose a previously created word processed document (with the extension WPS) in the Open Existing File dialog box.

THE SCREEN

When you're working with the Word Processor, you'll probably want to enlarge both the Works window and the document window by clicking the maximize button in the upper right corner of each window. In the illustration on the next page, both of these windows are maximized, and important elements are labeled.

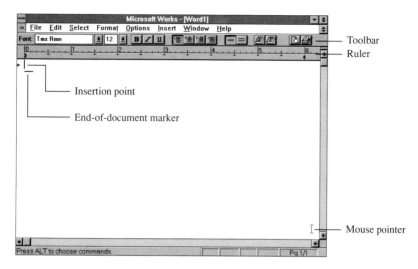

- The *Toolbar* gives you a quick way to carry out common commands with a mouse.

- The *ruler* helps you quickly indent paragraphs and set tabs with a mouse.

- The *insertion point,* a blinking vertical bar onscreen, shows where the next character you type will appear.

- The *end-of-document* marker shows onscreen where your file ends. You cannot move the insertion point beyond this marker.

- The *mouse pointer* shows what part of the screen your mouse is pointing to. The mouse pointer can take any of several forms. In the text area of a document window, it appears as an *I-beam.* In this form, illustrated in the previous figure, the mouse cursor lets you position the insertion point and select text.

In most locations outside the text area, the mouse cursor has the familiar arrow shape—for choosing, clicking, and dragging. On the split box at the top of the vertical scroll bar, it appears as a *split cursor,* which is used to split the screen for viewing different parts of a document.

ENTERING TEXT

If you've never used a word processor, you'll find it much like typing—only easier. Keep in mind the following difference, however: When you create a document, don't press Enter at the end of each line. The Works Word Processor, like all others of its kind, has a feature called *word wrap* that automatically begins a new line whenever a word would run into the margin of your printed page. Because of word wrap, the only time you press the Enter key is when you want to start a new paragraph.

Displaying Paragraph Marks

Unless you specify otherwise, the Word Processor typically displays your text as single-spaced block paragraphs. If you have difficulty distinguishing one paragraph from another, do the following:

1. Open the Options menu.

2. If a check mark doesn't appear next to Show All Characters, click on the menu item to turn this option on.

Show All Characters tells Works to display certain *nonprinting* characters, including spaces and paragraph marks. A ¶ symbol shows where each paragraph ends, as in the following sample document:

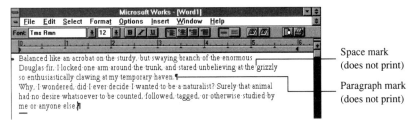

Space mark
(does not print)

Paragraph mark
(does not print)

Setting Off Your Paragraphs

When you print a document, Works doesn't print paragraph marks, so showing all characters distinguishes one paragraph from another onscreen but not necessarily on paper. One way to visually separate one paragraph from another is to press the Enter key twice at the end of a paragraph. Doing this produces a blank line between two paragraphs, both on the screen and in print.

Later sections of this chapter discuss other ways to tell the Word Processor how you want your paragraphs to look. This is called *formatting* the paragraph. The paragraphs illustrated on page 46, for example, are double-spaced with an extra line between them.

EDITING A DOCUMENT

Seldom, if ever, can even the best writer or the most accurate typist create a first draft that is also a finished draft. Somewhere between mind and machine, words trip over themselves, ideas get tangled, and letters or numbers decide to trade places. For whatever reason, mistakes happen, and fixing what you've typed becomes a way of life. The process of editing boils down to two steps:

- Selecting the text you want to edit
- Doing something to it (moving it, deleting it, or the like)

Moving Around in a Document

To select text, you must be able to find it, and finding text often requires that you look beyond the portion of your document that's currently displayed:

 Click in the scroll bars as necessary to view different parts of the document. Drag the scroll box to move more than one screenful at a time.

 Press PgDn or PgUp to move one screenful at a time. Press Ctrl-End or Ctrl-Home to move directly to the end or to the beginning of the document.

Once you have the insertion point in the general area you want, you can park it in a specific place by pointing and clicking with the mouse. You can also relocate the insertion point with the following keys:

Key or Combination	Moves the Cursor
Left or Right arrow key	Left or right one character
Up or Down arrow key	Up or down one line
End	To the end of the current line
Home	To the beginning of the current line
Ctrl-Left arrow	Left one word
Ctrl-Right arrow	Right one word
Ctrl-Up arrow	To the beginning of the previous paragraph
Ctrl-Down arrow	To the beginning of the following paragraph
Ctrl-PgUp	To the top of the window
Ctrl-PgDn	To the bottom of the window

Selecting Text

After you position the insertion point, select the text you want to edit. When you select text, the Word Processor shows what you've selected by highlighting it, as illustrated on the next page.

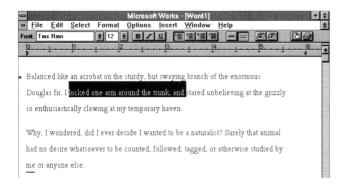

The following table lists ways to select text with the mouse or the keyboard (or a combination of the two). After you press F8 the first time (to select text elements with the keyboard), either finish your selection and edit it or press the Esc key to cancel the selection mode.

To Select the Following Text Element:		
Character	Drag the insertion point over the character	Press F8 and the Left or Right arrow key
Word	Double-click on the word	Press F8 two times
Line	Click in the margin at the left of the line	Press Home, F8, and then End
Sentence	Hold down Ctrl and click on the sentence	Press F8 three times
Paragraph	Double-click in the left margin	Press F8 four times
Whole document	Hold down Ctrl and click in the left margin	Press F8 five times

Undo

As you edit a document, you'll sometimes make a change and immediately recognize that you don't like it or didn't mean to make it. Whenever you want to backpedal, try the Undo command. Undo can reverse your last editing or formatting change. Unlike similar commands in other programs, the Works Undo command does not let you reverse the Undo command itself.

To use Undo,

■ Choose Undo from the Edit menu:

- Or press Alt-Backspace.

As soon as you choose Undo, the Word Processor reverses the last change you made. Remember, though, that the Undo command affects only the last change you made. If you try to choose Undo, but find that it's dimmed in the menu, there's nothing to undo—even though you might think there is.

Inserting Text

Works normally operates in *insert mode*, meaning that it moves existing text to the right as you type, to make room for new text. To insert any amount of new text,

1. Check the right side of the status bar. If you see *OVR* (short for *over-type*), press the Ins key to revert to insert mode.
2. Place the insertion point where you want it and begin typing.

Replacing Text

Although Works normally inserts new text, you can choose to have your new text replace existing text instead, either by overtyping it character by character or by replacing a selected block of text.

Overtyping

To overtype text, replacing one character with another,

1. Move the insertion point to the point at which you want to start replacing characters.
2. Turn on overtype mode by pressing the Ins key or by clicking Over-type on the Options menu. Either way, overtype is turned on when a check mark appears next to the Overtype option on the menu and the letters *OVR* appear in the status bar.

To turn off overtype mode, do either of the following:

- Press the Ins key a second time.
- Click Overtype on the Options menu to remove the check mark.

Overtyping is a one-to-one proposition, so it's fine for replacing *car* with *bus* because both contain the same number of letters. Overtyping *crocodile* with *bear*, however, would produce *bearodile*. Avoid creating bearodiles with the technique described next.

Swapping new text for old

To replace any amount of selected text with any amount of new text,

1. Select the text you want to replace.

2. Open the Options menu and verify that a check mark appears next to Typing Replaces Selection. If you don't see a check mark, click the option to turn it on. If it's already checked, click the menu name again or press the Esc key to close the menu.

3. Type whatever new text you want.

As soon as you begin typing, the selected text disappears and new text takes its place.

Deleting Text

You can delete text in a document two ways. To fix common typing errors, press the Backspace key to back over (erase) characters to the left of the insertion point, and then retype. To remove a significant block of existing text,

1. Select the text you want to delete.

2. Press the Del key or choose Delete from the Edit menu.

If you delete text and then decide you want it back, you can restore it with the Undo command, but be sure to do this before you make any other changes to your document.

Cut, Copy, and Paste

The Cut, Copy, and Paste commands use the Clipboard—a reserved portion of computer memory—as a temporary home for text you want to reuse. Cut and Copy move text to the Clipboard; Paste moves text from the Clipboard to a document. These commands let you reorganize a document with either of two techniques:

- Cut and paste, which *moves* a block of text.
- Copy and paste, which *duplicates* a block of text.

All three commands are on the Edit menu:

Cut and paste

Cut and paste is the best way to reorganize documents. With it, you can select, cut, and reinsert blocks of text as often as you want, anywhere in a document.

To cut and paste,

1. Select the text you want to cut. Remember, cutting removes the text from its current location.
2. Choose Cut from the Edit menu, or press Ctrl-X.
3. Move the insertion point to the place at which you want to insert the text you cut.
4. Choose Paste from the Edit menu, or press Ctrl-V.

NOTE: *The Edit menu offers both a Paste and a Paste Special command. Paste is a simple "put it here" command. Paste Special, on the other hand, lets you insert formats, rather than text, or insert information from another type of document, such as a spreadsheet. Chapter 10 tells more about Paste Special.*

Copy and paste

Copy and paste duplicates, rather than moves, text. Use copy and paste when you need to repeat text or repeat it with slight modification. Copy and paste can also be useful for "test editing" a passage for helping you decide whether a block of text fits better where it is or somewhere else.

To copy and paste,

1. Select the text you want to copy.

2. Choose Copy from the Edit menu, or press Ctrl-C.

3. Move the insertion point to the place at which you want to insert the text you copied.

4. Choose Paste from the Edit menu, or press Ctrl-V.

NOTE: *If you work with more than one Works application, you can copy from one document and paste what you've copied into a document in a different application. You'll find more about such interapplication moves in Chapter 10.*

CHECKING SPELLING AND FINDING SYNONYMS

Everyone occasionally stumbles over spelling. Even someone of presidential caliber might have difficulty remembering whether a hated vegetable is *broccoli* or *brocolli*. Finding the right word for a given situation can also be a struggle: Is there, for example, another word you can use for *thing*? Works can't always help, but very often, it can—and without costing you much effort. Ferreting out the correct word or spelling can be especially simple with the help of the Toolbar:

Spelling checker ⌐ ⌐ Thesaurus

Spelling

You can check your spelling whenever you want, and you can check as much text as you want, from a single word to an entire document.

■ To check part of a document, begin by highlighting the text you want to check.

■ To check the entire document, don't highlight a thing. You can leave the insertion point anywhere in the document, although starting at the beginning is nice and logical.

To start the spelling checker, do one of the following:

■ Click the spelling-checker button on the Toolbar.

■ Choose Check Spelling from the Options menu.

The spelling checker verifies the words in your document against the words in a 120,000-word dictionary. If it can't verify the spelling of a word, it highlights the word in text and displays a dialog box like this:

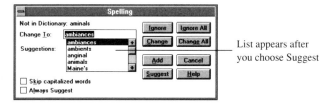

List appears after you choose Suggest

■ To list possible spellings, click the Suggest button. (This has already been done in the preceding illustration.)

■ To skip a "misspelled" (unverifiable) word, such as the proper name *Barton-Figby*, you can click Ignore to pass over the highlighted occurrence, click Ignore All to pass over all occurrences of that word in the document, or click Add to add the spelling to a personal dictionary Works will create for you.

■ To correct a spelling error, either type the correct version in the Change To box or choose it from the list of suggestions below. Then, click Change to correct the highlighted misspelling in text, or click Change All to change every occurrence of the misspelling throughout the document.

■ To skip capitalized words or automatically display a list of suggestions whenever the spelling checker finds a word it can't verify, turn on the appropriate check box at the bottom of the dialog box. Once on, these options remain in effect until you turn them off.

■ To quit the spelling checker, click the Cancel button. Any corrections you made before you quit will remain in the document.

Synonyms

The obvious use for the Thesaurus is finding synonyms, but this feature of the Word Processor also works as a handy, if terse, dictionary. To use the Thesaurus,

1. Place the insertion point anywhere in the word you want to look up.

2. Click the thesaurus button on the Toolbar or choose Thesaurus from the Options menu.

Asking for a synonym produces this dialog box:

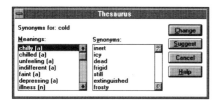

The Meanings box lists possible meanings for the word you chose (*cold*, in this example). The Synonyms box lists alternative words with the same meaning.

- To browse through different meanings, highlight another meaning and click Suggest.

- To find still more synonyms, highlight a word in the Synonyms box and click Suggest.

- To change the original word in text to a synonym, highlight the meaning or synonym you want and click Change.

FORMATTING

Word processing offers one great advantage over a typewriter when you begin defining the way your document looks. At any time before, during, or after you've written and revised your text, you can experiment with different formats for words, paragraphs, page margins, tab stops, and other niceties that can turn a good document into a visually inviting one. Document formatting breaks down into three major categories: formatting the character, the paragraph, and the page.

Formatting Characters

There are two sides to character formatting: The first includes the shape and size of the characters themselves, and the second comprises any additional styling you apply, such as italic, boldfacing, or underlining.

Fonts

The term *font* refers to the design of the characters you use in a document. Fonts always have names, such as Courier or Prestige Elite, and they come in different sizes, measured in points. The sizes range from very small to—potentially—headline size. All fonts are not available in the same sizes, however, nor are all possible fonts available to you. Printers (the machines, not the people) differ in the number, kinds, and sizes of fonts they can reproduce, so the fonts and font sizes from which you can choose are determined entirely by the type of printer you've connected to your computer.

Fortunately, you don't need to serve as a typesetter's apprentice to find out what fonts and font sizes you have available. Works, through Windows, is able to gather all the font and size information it needs about your printer; it displays available fonts and sizes both in the Toolbar and in a Font & Style dialog box you reach from the Format menu.

Applying fonts

You can change fonts and font sizes at any time. To enter characters of a specific font and size, place the insertion point where you want the change to begin, select the font and size you want, and then type the characters. To affect a block of existing text, select the text before choosing a font and font size.

To change fonts and sizes, you can use either the Toolbar or the Font & Style command on the Format menu.

With the Toolbar,

1. Click on the down arrow to the right of the Font box; from the list displayed, click on the name of the font you want.

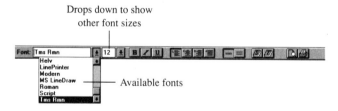

2. If you want a different font size, click on the down arrow to the right of the size box and choose the size.

With the Format menu,

1. Choose the Font & Style command. Works produces the dialog box shown at the top of the next page.

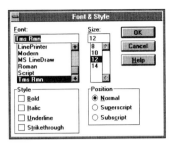

2. Click on the font and, if appropriate, the size you want. Click OK to carry out the command.

Font styles

In addition to fonts and font sizes, you can apply, remove, mix, and match a number of different *font styles*. In addition to **bold**, *italic*, and underline, you can use ~~strikethrough~~ characters for editing. You can also use superscript and subscript characters in footnotes and formulas such as $E=mc^2$ and H_2O.

You can use the buttons labeled below to apply boldfacing, italics, and underlining to your text:

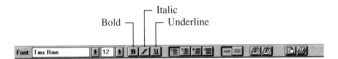

To apply these styles, as well as other font styles not available on the Toolbar, click the appropriate check boxes or buttons in the Font & Style dialog box, or use the following key combinations:

Font Style	Keyboard Shortcut
Boldfacing	Ctrl-B
Italics	Ctrl-I
Subscripting	Ctrl-equal sign (Ctrl-=)
Superscripting	Ctrl-plus (Ctrl-Shift-+)
Underlining	Ctrl-U

To remove a font style or to stop applying it to your typing, do one of the following:

- Click in the Toolbar to "unpress" the button applying the style.
- Choose the Font & Style command from the format menu. Deselect the style.

■ Press Ctrl-Spacebar. (This removes *all* special font styles you've applied.)

Formatting Paragraphs

Whereas fonts and character styles affect the look of individual characters, *paragraph formats* affect the look of blocks of text:

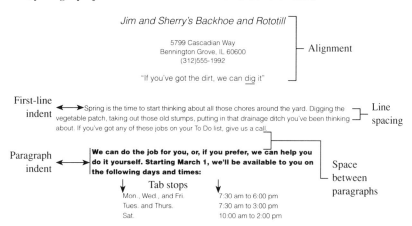

To apply a particular format to the paragraph you are typing, simply specify the format you want, as described in the following sections. As you type successive paragraphs, Works applies the same format. To apply a particular format to one or more existing paragraphs, select the paragraphs and then define the format.

In using the Word Processor, remember that you create a new paragraph whenever you press the Enter key. Furthermore, it's the paragraph mark produced by pressing Enter that controls the alignment, spacing, and other features of the paragraph.

Paragraph alignment

Paragraph alignment refers to the positioning of the lines in relation to the margins of your page. With Works, a paragraph can have any of the alignments shown in the screen at the top of the next page.

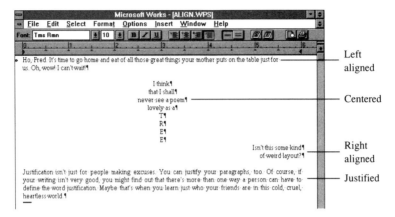

You can align paragraphs with these buttons on the Toolbar:

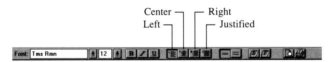

Or you can use the Indents & Spacing command on the Format menu. Choose the type of alignment you want from the resulting dialog box:

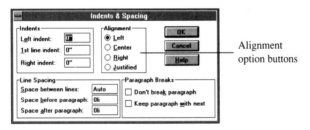

You can also use the following keyboard shortcuts to align paragraphs:

Alignment	Keyboard Shortcut
Left	Ctrl-L
Center	Ctrl-E
Right	Ctrl-R
Justified	Ctrl-J
Normal	Ctrl-Q

First-line and paragraph indents

A *first-line indent* pushes the first line of each paragraph farther toward the right than succeeding lines. If you don't use extra line spaces to separate paragraphs, you normally give each one a first-line indent.

A *paragraph indent* determines whether all the lines of the paragraph are indented farther toward the center of the page than the amount set by the left and right margins. Paragraph indents are useful for setting off quotations and other text you want to call attention to, like this:

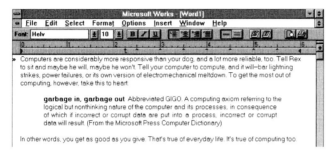

If you have a mouse, you can set indents directly onscreen by dragging any of three small markers on the ruler:

Drag the first-line indent marker to indent the
first line of a paragraph from the left margin.

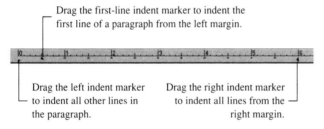

Drag the left indent marker
to indent all other lines in
the paragraph.

Drag the right indent marker
to indent all lines from the
right margin.

If you don't have a mouse or if you want to set very precise indents, use the Indents & Spacing command:

1. From the Format menu, choose Indents & Spacing, which produces a dialog box.

2. Type the measurements you want in the box labeled Indents.

Nested paragraphs

A *nested paragraph* is indented beneath the paragraph above it. To create a nested paragraph quickly, press Ctrl-N. Each time you press Ctrl-N, Works indents the paragraph one-half inch farther from the left margin. To undo nesting (one-half inch at a time), press Ctrl-M.

You can also create nested paragraphs by

■ Dragging the left indent marker to the required position on the ruler

■ Specifying the left indent with the Indents & Spacing command

For information on another special paragraph alignment called a *hanging indent,* refer to the section "Hanging Indents" later in this chapter.

Line spacing and space between paragraphs

Line spacing refers to the amount of space between the lines in the body of the paragraph. In addition to the usual single-spacing and double-spacing, you can customize paragraphs by spacing the text a particular number of lines apart. If you want, you can specify the separation in inches, centimeters, picas, or points.

Space between paragraphs refers to the amount of space above or below each paragraph. Space between paragraphs is commonly used to set off paragraphs that have no first-line indent. Varying the spacing between paragraphs can produce some interesting printed effects, such as the following (shown here in Print Preview mode):

To set line spacing, you can use the Toolbar or the Indents & Spacing command. The Indents & Spacing command gives you more spacing options than you get with the Toolbar.

With the Toolbar, you can click the single-space or double-space buttons to change the spacing of the current paragraph or selected paragraphs:

In the Indents & Spacing dialog box (shown earlier on page 56), you can set both line spacing and space between paragraphs:

■ Type the value you want for Space Between Lines. You can specify the spacing as a number of lines, such as *1.5*, or you can specify the distance between lines as a measurement by including some unit of measure—for example, *.25 in.* The default, *Auto*, means that lines are single-spaced (with a little fine-tuning to ensure that the spacing is appropriate for the largest font in the line).

■ To add extra space above or below paragraphs, type a number to specify lines. Follow the number with a unit of measure if you want to specify the distance in inches, centimeters, or some other measure.

Use the following keyboard shortcuts to change the spacing of high-lighted lines or paragraphs in a document.

Spacing	Keyboard Shortcut
Single-spacing	Ctrl-1
Double-spacing	Ctrl-2
1.5 lines apart	Ctrl-5
Closed-up before paragraph	Ctrl-0 (zero)
Opened-up before paragraph	Ctrl-O (letter O)

Hanging indents

You can use indents and tabs to produce a *hanging indented* paragraph format in which the first line is *outdented,* and the remaining lines ''hang'' beneath it. Hanging indents are commonly used for itemized or numbered lists and are created by setting a left indent and a negative first-line indent. The following illustration shows two types of hanging indent. The first you can create simply with a keyboard shortcut; the other you can create with the ruler or with the Indents & Spacing command:

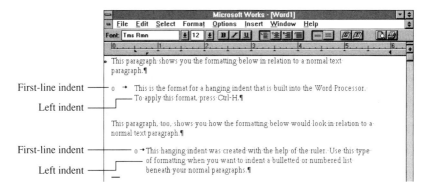

To use the keyboard,

■ Press Ctrl-H to create the hanging indent.

■ Press Ctrl-G to remove the hanging indent format.

To create a customized hanging indent,

1. Set the left indent with the ruler or with the Indents & Spacing command.

2. Set the first-line indent either by dragging the ruler's first-line indent marker *to the left,* to the place where you want the outdented line to

begin, or by choosing the Indents & Spacing command and typing a *negative* value for the first-line indent—for example, type −.5 for one-half inch *less* than the left indent for the rest of the paragraph.

Regardless of the method you use, you create entries with the hanging indent in the same way: Type the bullet character or the number you want outdented, press Tab to move to the left indent, and then start typing. Your formatting will align the paragraph correctly.

Tabs

Tab stops are the means you use to align text vertically on the page. You can use tabs to set special indents or to create columns of text, as in a table. (You can also create tables by copying from the Spreadsheet with the Copy and Paste commands.)

The Word Processor normally assumes that tab stops occur every one-half inch across the page. You can change this default setting and you can set several types of tab stops: left aligned, centered, right aligned, or aligned on the decimal point. You can also specify a *leader* character if you want to fill the blank space leading to the tab stop with a series of characters—typically dots, dashes, or the like. Tab alignments and two samples with leaders are shown and labeled in the following illustration. Notice that the tab indicators on the ruler show the kind of alignment for each tab stop.

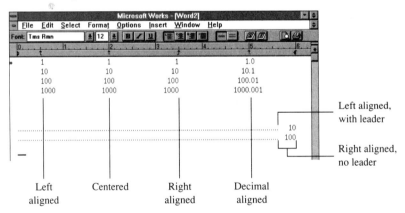

You can set left-aligned tab stops simply by clicking on the appropriate place on the ruler. For other types of tab stops, use the Tabs command on the Format menu:

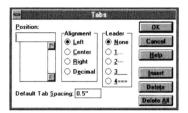

1. In the Position box, type the location of the tab stop—for example, *.75* to set a tab 0.75 inch from the left margin.

2. Click the type of alignment you want.

3. Click the leader character, if any, that you want.

4. To set multiple tab stops, click the Insert button in the Tabs dialog box after specifying each tab setting. When you finish, click OK.

To delete tab stops, do either of the following:

■ Drag each one off the ruler with the mouse.

■ Choose the Tabs command, click on the tab-stop position you want to delete, and click Delete. Delete all tab stops in a paragraph by choosing the Tabs command and clicking Delete All.

Defining Page Layouts

Page layout refers to all the elements that affect every page of your document: margins, page numbers, and so on. If you use Works exactly as it comes out of the box, your word processed documents will have top and bottom margins of 1 inch and left and right margins of 1.25 inches each. For business documents in particular, you might find that a 1-inch top margin is too small, especially if you want to print a name, a date, a page number, or other *header* information in the top margin. If you prefer to see this type of information at the bottom of the page as a *footer,* you'll probably want to increase the bottom margin.

Headers and footers

Headers and footers are lines of text that repeat on each page of a printed document. Headers are more common than footers, but you can use either or both in a document to identify the author, the recipient (of a letter, for example), the date, the page number, and so on. You can create headers and footers with the (of course) Headers & Footers command on the Edit menu. When you choose this command, Works displays the dialog box at the top of the next page.

Although it isn't immediately obvious, this dialog box indicates that you can insert headers and footers in either of two ways:

■ By typing into the text boxes labeled Header and Footer. This creates *standard* headers and footers.

■ By turning on the option Use Header And Footer Paragraphs. This creates header and footer *paragraphs,* as opposed to the standard items.

Standard headers and footers The standard format is ideal for simple, one-line headers and footers. To create a standard header or footer,

1. Choose the Headers & Footers command. Verify that Use Head And Footer Paragraphs is not checked.

2. Type the text of your header or footer. You can align (subsequent) text and insert special information by typing one of the following codes:

Code	Purpose
&L	Left-align subsequent text
&C	Center-align subsequent text
&R	Right-align subsequent text
&P	Print page number
&F	Print filename
&D	Print date in short form (12/9/92 in U.S. format)
&N	Print date in long form (December 9, 1992 in U.S. format)
&T	Print time (3:39 PM in U.S. format)
&&	Print an ampersand

The following example shows a standard header and codes:

The result, which you can see with the Print Preview feature (described under ''Printing'') looks like this:

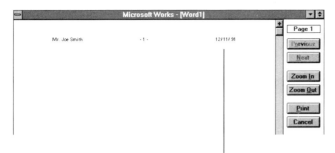

The codes &R&D right-align the date
(in short form) with the right margin.

Unless you use one of the alignment codes, Works centers a standard
header or footer.

Header and footer paragraphs Header and footer paragraphs are your
ticket for multiple lines of text or for the inclusion of illustrations
(created with a drawing program) in your headers or footers. To create
header and footer paragraphs,

1. Choose the Headers & Footers command.

2. Click to turn on Use Header And Footer Paragraphs, and then click
   OK.

When you return to your document, you'll notice that Works displays
two special paragraphs at the top:

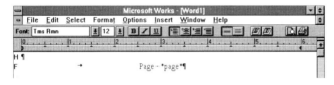

If you don't want a footer paragraph, select the text and delete it. Works
won't let you delete the paragraph itself, but deleting the text is equivalent to saying, "OK, so print a footer with nothing in it."

By default, the header paragraph (labeled H) has a centered tab and a
right-aligned tab. To use these settings,

1. Type any text you want at the left side of the header.

2. Press Tab and type the text you want centered.

3. Press Tab again and type the text you want right aligned.

4. To create a multiple-line header paragraph, press Shift-Enter to begin
   a new line. Do *not* press Enter.

With header and footer paragraphs, you do not use the ampersand and letter codes to align text or to insert special information, such as page numbers. Set tabs to align text. To insert page numbers and other information, use the Special Character command on the Insert menu:

Choose the special character you want. When Works displays it onscreen, you'll see a text description surrounded by asterisks (*) as in the text *Page - *page** that Works inserts as a default footer line. As you do for standard headers and footers, use the Print Preview feature to see what your actual printed text will look like.

NOTE: *The Special Character command is not limited to use in headers and footers. You can also use it to insert special characters anywhere in a word processed document. For descriptions of the other characters, such as non-breaking hyphens, click the Help button in the Special Character dialog box.*

If you create a header or footer that is too deep to fit into the top or bottom margin of the page, Works warns you of the problem when you try to print or preview your document. If you see such a message, cancel your command and use the Page Setup & Margins command described in the next section.

Page setup and margins

The Page Setup & Margins command on the File menu lets you alter any of the settings in the dialog box that follows. To change any of these values, type your preferred setting in the appropriate text box.

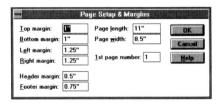

The settings for Header margin and Footer margin indicate how far from the top and bottom edges of the page Works will print header and footer text. If Works has warned you that a multiple-line header is too tall, for example, either type a smaller value for the header margin or increase the size of the top margin. Of these alternatives, increasing the margin is probably the better choice to produce a well-spaced, uncrowded document.

Two important settings in the Page Setup & Margins dialog box are the Page Length and Page Width text boxes. In these two boxes, Works displays the paper size it expects your printer to be using. If you want to change to a different paper size, type the new measurements here. For example, to switch to legal-size (8.5" by 14") paper, type *14* in the Page Length box.

Page length and width are *not* the same as page orientation. Some printers can print in either *portrait* or *landscape* orientation:

Portrait   Landscape

If your printer has this capability and you want to change orientation,

1. Switch the page length and width in the Page Setup & Margins dialog box. Click OK.

2. Choose the Printer Setup command and select the orientation you want.

PRINTING

When it comes to printing the results of your work, you never have to worry about surprises. The Word Processor is a *WYSIWYG* program. WYSIWYG (pronounced "wizzywig") stands for What You See Is What You Get—the Word Processor shows you onscreen what your document will look like on paper. As you type, Works displays screen characters (called a screen font) that match the ultimate printed version as closely as possible. Italics look like italics and large type is displayed in correspondingly large characters. Furthermore, the Word Processor can also save time and paper by letting you preview the document a page at a time onscreen before you send it to your printer.

Printer Setup

When Works is installed on your computer, it finds out about your printer through Windows. In fact, if you try to install a new printer, add new fonts, or otherwise redefine a printer while using Works, Works turns the job over to Windows. To gain access to printer information and perform any type of setup task (setup tasks are seen as distinct from installation), you can use the Printer Setup command on the Works File menu. Through this command, you can do such things as

■ Choose a different (previously installed) printer

■ Specify a different paper tray, paper size, or page orientation

■ Choose the number of dots per inch (dpi) that your printer (if capable) will use in printing graphics, such as those you create with Microsoft Draw

Whenever you choose the Printer Setup command, you see a dialog box that, in turn, can contain buttons that lead to other, more specific options. The contents of the dialog boxes themselves vary, depending on the make and model of your printer. Because printer setups are variable, your best sources of advice are

■ The Help button in the Printer Setup dialog box

■ Your printer manual

Aside from changing paper trays and page orientation, you probably won't need the Printer Setup command often.

Print Preview

One of Works' most appealing features is its ability to show you onscreen what your printed document will look like. This capability, Print Preview, is accessible either through the Toolbar, as shown below, or through the Print Preview command on the File menu.

When you choose to preview a document, you see a screen like this:

To get a closer look at your document,

1. Click anywhere on the ''page'' or click the Zoom In button.

2. Repeat the process to zoom in even closer.

Use the scroll bars to see different parts of a zoomed page. When you're ready to zoom out after a closeup, click on the ''page'' or click the Zoom Out button.

To move to different pages in a multiple-page document, click the Previous and Next buttons. If you're satisfied with the look of the document, you can print directly from Print Preview by clicking the Print button. You can also return to normal view by clicking Cancel.

Pagination and Printing

In the background, the Word Processor counts lines as you type and automatically breaks to a new page whenever necessary. You can see your page breaks onscreen by checking the left margin for a small double arrowhead >>. As you scan for page breaks, you can change any you don't like. For example, if a page break occurs at an awkward place in a paragraph or a table, you can move the page break up. To do this,

1. Place the insertion point in front of the first character to appear on the new page.

2. Choose Page Break from the Insert menu, or press Ctrl-Enter.

When you insert a page break, the Word Processor shows it onscreen as a row of closely spaced dots. To check pagination in the remainder of the document,

1. Choose Paginate Now from the Options menu.

2. Scroll through the document in normal view or in Print Preview.

When you're satisfied with your document, you can print it in any of the following ways:

■ Click the Print button in the Toolbar.

■ Choose Print from the File menu.

■ Click the Print button in Print Preview.

■ Press Ctrl-P.

After you issue the Print command, you see this dialog box appear:

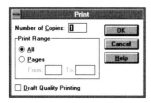

■ If you want more than one copy, type the number in the Number Of Copies box.

■ If you want to print specific pages, click Pages in the Print Range box. Type the number of the first page you want to print in the From box, and type the number of the last page in the To box.

■ If a quick draft copy will do, check the Draft Quality Printing box. A draft copy does not show different fonts and excludes graphics, although you will see blank spaces where the graphics will appear in a nondraft copy.

CHAPTER 5

Draw Basics

Putting a picture into a word processed document used to be a little easier than putting an omelet back into its shell. These days, working with graphics is, by comparison, a piece of cake. Thanks to Works, you have an easy-to-use onscreen drawing pad on which you can create a picture and from which you can move a drawing into your document. Your drawing program is Microsoft Draw, and because it works with the Word Processor in Works, you'll find much of it immediately familiar. In this chapter, you'll see how to

- Start Draw
- Use clip art
- Use the drawing tools
- Edit drawings
- Move a drawing to a word processed document
- Return to Draw when you want to modify a drawing

WHAT CAN DRAW DRAW?

Asking what Draw can draw might seem like a stupid question, but it isn't really. Illustration programs for computers come in two basic varieties, generally called *drawing* programs and *painting* programs. Draw is a drawing program, which means that it treats each separate element you draw as an *object*—a single shape that you can manipulate simply by selecting it. When you work with Draw, you treat the objects in your drawing as if they were paper cutouts. That means you can selectively grab objects and move, flip, copy, color, overlap, or delete them with ease.

In contrast, a painting program, such as the Windows Paintbrush accessory, treats a drawing as a collection of *pixels*—dots that you can manipulate singly, but not necessarily in groups. Painting programs treat your pictures as if they were made of grains of sand. Because of this, you can alter a drawing on a dot-by-dot basis for precision and creative flair, but you can't pick a single shape out of a painting and move it, nor can you place one shape on top of another without altering the one below.

Which is better? Drawing programs are easier to use, especially when you're interested in creating geometric designs. Painting programs afford you a better chance to satisfy your artistic muse. Although the Works Word Processor is designed to work with Draw, it can also accept images from Paintbrush, so you've really got the best of both worlds.

NOTE: *This chapter is only about using Draw. You can find plenty of help with Paintbrush, however, by starting the program from the Windows Accessories group and browsing through its Help topics.*

STARTING DRAW

To start Draw you begin by opening or creating a document with the Word Processor. Even if you want only a drawing, with no text, open a new document. You can't move to Draw directly from the Startup dialog box or by choosing an existing file, so

1. Start the Word Processor with the document in which you want to include a drawing.

2. Choose Drawing from the Insert menu.

In a few moments, your Word Processor window is overlaid with a new Draw window, as shown in Figure 5-1. The Draw window contains two sets of tools: a *Toolbox* of drawing tools running down the left side of the Draw window and two *palettes* running across the bottom.

Most of the Draw window is familiar territory, but because of the relationship between Draw and the Word Processor, the Draw title bar displays the name of the word processed document to which Works will *export* your drawing. In a sense, your drawing exists only in the Word Processor, even though you work on it in Draw.

You should know, by the way, that when you export a drawing to a word processed document, the drawing becomes an *embedded object*—one that you view and print in one application (the Word Processor) but create and modify in another (Draw). You don't have to know any more than that about embedding, but the terminology is useful to remember because you encounter references to objects and embedded objects in menus and in Works Help.

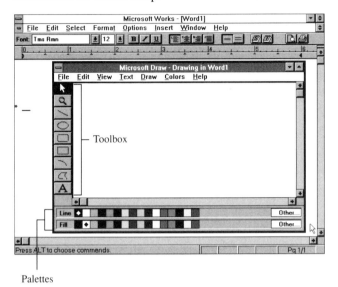

Toolbox

Palettes

FIGURE 5-1. *Even though you start Draw from the Word Processor, Draw is a separate application and opens in an application window of its own.*

USING CLIP ART

When you're working with pen or pencil, sketching onto a sheet of paper is easy. When you're working with Draw, artwork takes a little more practice because you use the mouse to "pick up" and manipulate your drawing tools. You have to become accustomed to moving your entire hand, not merely your fingers, as you work. If you just can't get the hang of it, or if you prefer to rely on a better artist than yourself, you can often *import* an appropriate image from the collection of clip art that comes with Works.

The clip art library resides in the CLIPART subdirectory within the MSWORKS directory. To see a list of clip art designs,

1. Choose Import Picture from Draw's File menu. When you do, Works opens the dialog box on the next page.

2. Double-click *[clipart]* in the Directories list box. If you don't see the CLIPART directory, Works (and Draw) are currently focused on a different directory. Change to the MSWORKS directory, and you'll see CLIPART listed as one of its subdirectories.

When you open the CLIPART directory, Draw displays the beginning of a long list of clip art images. To see the list and choose an image:

1. Click the vertical scroll bar or tab to the Files box and use the PgDn and PgUp keys.

2. Double-click the image you want, or highlight its name and press Enter.

As soon as you choose an image, the dialog box disappears and a picture appears in the Draw window:

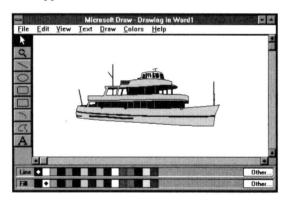

USING THE DRAWING TOOLS

As useful and entertaining as clip art can be, you might sometimes need a customized piece of artwork, such as a logo for your company, your school, or an organization to which you belong. You can create your own design in a couple of ways.

- Modify a clip art image.
- Draw the design from scratch.

Either way, you'll need the help of Draw's drawing tools—the Toolbox, the palettes, and the Draw menus.

Drawing Shapes

The Draw Toolbox offers an assortment of nine tools, most of which help you draw geometric shapes. To select the tool you want to use, point to the tool and click. Doing so highlights the tool and removes the highlight from any previously selected tool.

The tools and the basic shapes are shown and labeled below:

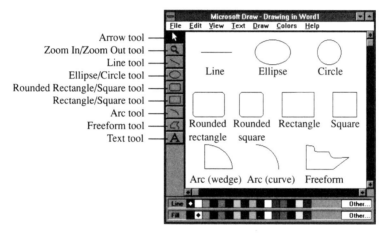

The Arrow tool

Acting somewhat like the mouse pointer, the Arrow tool helps you select an object. To use it, simply point to what you want and click.

The Arrow tool is also handy if you merely want to *deselect* another tool, and it's the tool Draw will take you back to when you've finished with another tool.

The Zoom In/Zoom Out tool

Like the Zoom buttons in Print Preview, this tool changes magnification by zooming in or out. The Zoom tool affects your entire drawing, not only the selected object. You can zoom in to 200%, 400%, or 800% of full size, or zoom out to 75%, 50%, or 25% of full size:

- To zoom in, click anywhere in the document window.
- To zoom out, hold down the Shift key and click.

- To cycle through different magnifications, click (or Shift-click) repeatedly.

The Line tool

Select the Line tool to draw several types of straight lines:

- To draw a line from one end to the other, as if you were using a pencil, position the pointer where you want the line to start and drag the mouse.

- To draw a line from the center out toward both ends, hold down Ctrl while you drag.

- To draw a line that's exactly vertical, horizontal, or slanted at a 45-degree angle, hold down Shift while you drag.

- To draw a line from the center out, at an angle that is some multiple of 45 degrees, hold down both Ctrl and Shift while you drag.

Tools for drawing rounded and rectangular shapes

The next three tools in the Toolbox help you draw ellipses, circles, rectangles, and squares. You can draw any of these shapes in either of the ways shown below: from one corner (or point on the curve) to its opposite, or from the center outward. In the illustration, the arrows inside the rectangles represent cursor movement; those outside the rectangles indicate the expansion of the sides.

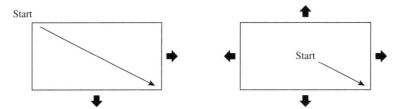

In general, these rules apply:

- To draw a shape from one end to the other, drag the mouse as usual.

- To draw a shape from the center outward, hold down Ctrl while you drag.

The following sections give you more details.

The Ellipse/Circle tool Choose the Ellipse/Circle tool to draw ellipses or circles, depending on what keys you press:

- Drag the mouse to draw an ellipse from one end.

- Hold down Ctrl while dragging to draw an ellipse from its center.

■ Hold down Shift while dragging to draw a circle from one end.

■ Hold down both Ctrl and Shift while dragging to draw a circle from its center.

The Rounded Rectangle/Square tool Choose the Rounded Rectangle/Square tool to draw rectangles and squares with rounded corners:

■ Drag the mouse to draw a rounded rectangle from one corner.

■ Hold down Ctrl while dragging to draw a rounded rectangle from its center.

■ Hold down Shift while dragging to draw a square with rounded corners.

■ Hold down both Ctrl and Shift while dragging to draw a square from its center.

The Rectangle/Square tool The Rectangle/Square tool works exactly like the Rounded Rectangle/Square tool, except that it produces rectangles and squares with sharp, rather than rounded, corners. Draw these figures as described above.

The Arc tool

The Arc tool draws 90-degree segments (quarters) of ellipses and circles. Depending on your choice of the settings described later under the heading ''Frames and Fillings,'' you can create arcs that are either solid wedges like large pieces of pie or plain, curved lines that resemble half a rainbow. To draw an arc,

■ Drag the mouse at an angle to form part of an ellipse.

■ Hold down Shift as you drag to form part of a circle.

The Freeform tool

Choose the Freeform tool to draw polygons and irregular shapes:

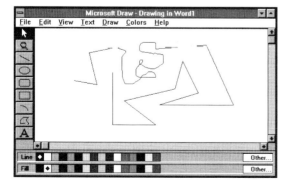

The type of line you draw depends on what you do:

- Click on two points to draw a straight line between those points. When you're drawing straight lines, the mouse pointer retains the appearance of a large plus sign.

- Drag the mouse to draw a freeform line (squiggle). When you're drawing like this, the pointer is shaped like a small pencil.

With each successive click, the starting point for the next line jumps to the ending point of the previous segment. In this way, you can add line after line to a freeform shape. When you're finished, you can join the end to the beginning and create a closed figure by moving the pointer close to your starting point and clicking. Draw will connect the last line with the first.

If you want to create an open-ended figure instead, double-click, press Esc, or press Enter when you finish the last line. Don't forget how to terminate your freeform shapes, or you can find yourself unreeling new lines whenever you click, like a demented spider.

The Text tool

Choose the Text tool to add text to a drawing. When you do so, Draw treats whatever text you type in a single line as an object, so you can treat a group of letters as if they were sitting inside an invisible box — drag them around the screen, perhaps, or place them inside a circle or other geometric shape.

To add text,

1. Choose the font, font size, font styles, and alignment (with respect to the insertion point) you want. Don't worry about getting this completely right. You can select the text object later and change any of these features if you want.

2. Choose the Text tool, position the pointer on the screen, and click. Because you can move the text around on the screen, any clear area will do.

3. When the blinking insertion point appears, type the text you want — one line only. When you finish, click somewhere else in the document window, press Enter, or press Esc.

Because Draw treats letters as objects, you can work with text in two ways: by typing a line of text that you want to handle as a single object, or by typing individual letters as separate objects. If you make each letter an object in its own right, you can arrange letters in patterns or combine differently sized letters, as in a monogram.

USING STYLES, PATTERNS, AND COLOR

The horizontal *palettes* at the bottom of the Draw window display rows of colors (on a color monitor) from which you can choose. The upper row, the Line palette, affects text and the outline, or *frame*, of a shape you draw. The lower row, the Fill palette, determines the interior color, or *fill*, of a shape. If you use colors, they are, of course, printable only if you have a color printer. You can use a variety of frames and fills—whether you introduce color into your drawing or not—by altering the line style or the fill pattern. You can also eliminate frames or fills altogether, if you want.

Frames and Fills

Because Draw distinguishes between the frame of a shape and its fill, you can combine these two features in three ways, as shown below. Of course, a fourth combination does exist—unframed and unfilled—but it isn't included here; eliminating both the frame and the fill effectively makes an object invisible.

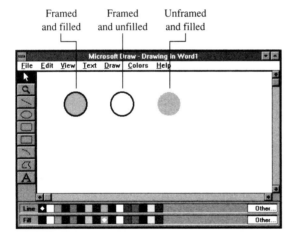

To set the frame and fill for your drawings, do the following:

1. Open the Draw menu.

2. If a checkmark or a diamond does not appear next to Framed, click the option to turn it on.

3. If a checkmark or a diamond does not appear next to Filled, click to turn this option on.

NOTE: *In Draw, a diamond indicates the current default setting. A checkmark indicates the setting for the currently selected object or objects. You see diamonds and checkmarks in the palettes as well as in menus.*

Patterns and Line Styles

Normally, Draw uses thin, solid lines as frames and solid colors (including white) as fills. You can change to thicker lines or more exotic combinations with the Pattern and Line Style options on the Draw menu. Using these options, you can produce effects such as these:

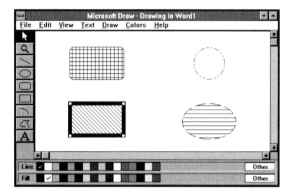

To change the fill from solid to a striped or checkerboard pattern,

1. Choose Pattern from the Draw menu. When you do, the following submenu opens:

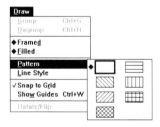

2. Click the pattern you want. The new pattern won't affect any existing objects you've drawn unless they're currently selected, but it will be used for any objects you create from this time on.

To change the line style of your frames,

1. Choose Line Style from the Draw menu. Draw opens the following submenu:

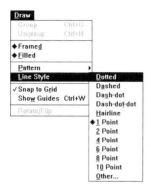

2. Click one of the dot and dash combinations to create a broken-line border, or click one of the point sizes to change the thickness of the border. (Click Other and type a point size if the one you want is not listed.) Line styles are mutually exclusive. You cannot, for example, choose a 10-point border that is also dashed and dotted.

Palettes

The color palettes at the bottom of the Draw window are your means of changing line and text colors, as well as the color of an object's frame, fill, or both. When you change the frame or fill color, the change affects subsequent objects you draw, but not any that currently exist in your drawing unless they are selected.

■ To change the color of lines, text, and frames (as well as the foreground if you've chosen a fill pattern), click the color you want in the Line palette.

■ To change the fill color (the background if you've chosen a fill pattern), click the color you want in the Fill palette.

Changing palettes

Draw comes with a set of palettes you can choose from, including one that offers varying shades of gray. To change palettes,

1. Open the Colors menu and choose Get Palette, which displays the dialog box on the next page.

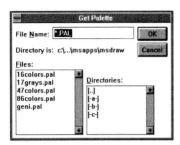

2. Double-click the palette you want. The Line and Fill palettes will both change to display the colors in your new palette.

The palette named 16COLORS.PAL contains 16 solid colors; it's the one that normally appears at the bottom of your Draw window. The palette 17GRAYS.PAL contains a selection of grays. 47COLORS.PAL, 86COLORS.PAL, and GENI.PAL expand your selection considerably. If you use these palettes, you'll notice that many colors are *dithered*—they are created using patterns of different-colored dots. Dithering occurs when a color can't be accurately reproduced as a solid by Draw or by your computer.

NOTE: *In addition to changing palettes, you can edit or create your own custom colors. You can find information on this procedure under Using Color in the Help Index.*

EDITING DRAWINGS

Lines, patterns, and colors are only the beginning; you'll find many other ways to work with a drawing. Thanks to Draw's flexibility, you can move, resize, copy, paste, flip, overlap, and group objects in a drawing. Note too that you can edit clip art as well as your own creations.

Moving Objects

When you draw, chances are that somewhere down the line you'll want to move objects around on the screen. To move an object, you select it and drag it to a new location. You can select and move a single object, or you can corral a group of objects and move them all:

■ To select a single object, point to it and click.

■ To select a group of objects, select the Arrow tool, place the mouse pointer near the objects, and drag to enclose them all in a dotted line:

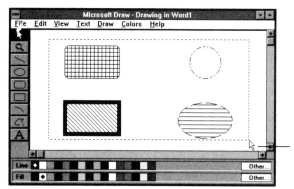

To select a group of objects, click and drag with the Arrow tool to enclose the objects within a dashed rectangle.

■ To select multiple objects that don't fit neatly within a selection rectangle, click on the first object and then hold down the Shift key while you click on each of the other objects.

Whether you select one object or several, you'll notice that Draw displays small, dark squares around each object. These squares are called *resize handles*.

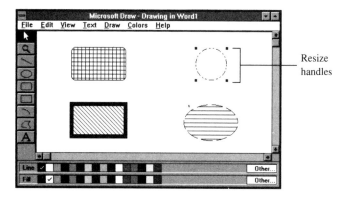

Resize handles

To move an object or group of objects, point to some part of the object *other than* the resize handles and drag. If the object is framed but not filled, be sure to place the pointer on the frame. If you point to the middle of an unfilled circle or other shape, you won't be able to "grab" and move it.

When you move an object, you'll see a dotted outline follow the mouse pointer as you drag. If you drag a group of objects slowly (*very* slowly in many instances) you'll see moving outlines of each object in the group. If you drag such a group quickly, however, you simply see a group-sized rectangle following the mouse pointer.

Resizing an Object

To change the size of an object, point to one of the resize handles and drag in the direction you want the object to grow or shrink:

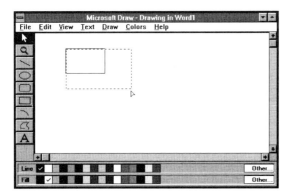

You can use the resize handles only with "pictures," not with text. To resize text, select it and then use the Font and Size commands on the Text menu.

Editing Objects

Just as you can edit text and copy it to and from the Clipboard in the Word Processor, you can edit and move objects in Draw. Because Works applications are so consistent, most of the commands you need are either familiar or self-explanatory. Cut, Copy, and Paste, for instance, work as they do in the Word Processor. If you want a refresher on these commands, either refer to Chapter 4, or choose Menu Commands from the Help menu and go to the Help topic you need.

Of Guides and Grids

If you want to move objects with precision, choose the Show Guides command from the Draw menu to display a set of movable dotted lines you can use for aligning objects. If objects you move seem to jump from one place to another, especially when the guides are visible, Draw is "snapping" them to an invisible grid for alignment. To position objects more smoothly, move or eliminate the guides and turn off Snap to Grid on the Draw menu. If you need more information on these topics, choose Menu Commands on the Help menu.

Other commands that help you manipulate objects are

■ Clear, which deletes a selected object without sending it to the Clipboard. Clear is available only when one or more objects are selected.

■ Select All, which selects all the objects in your drawing. Remember this command when you want to erase everything on your Draw sketchpad and start over.

■ Bring to Front and Send to Back, which move the selected object to the front or back of a "stack." Use this command when you've overlapped objects and you want to alter their foreground-background relationships, like this:

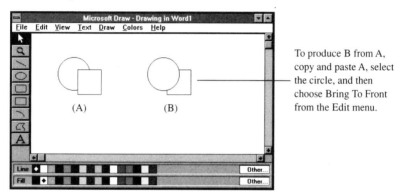

To produce B from A, copy and paste A, select the circle, and then choose Bring To Front from the Edit menu.

■ Edit [object], which is active when you've selected an arc or a freeform. When you use this command, small boxes called *control handles* appear at the vertices of the selected arc or freeform. You can drag these handles to reshape the line segments between the box and its adjacent boxes. (A quick way to cause the control handles of an arc or freeform to appear is simply to double-click on the arc or freeform.)

Rotating and Flipping Objects

Rotate/Flip (on the Draw menu) is a "special-effects" type of command that can help you change the orientation of objects you draw. To use it,

1. Select the object.

2. Choose Rotate/Flip from the Draw menu. When you do this, a small submenu opens as shown on the next page.

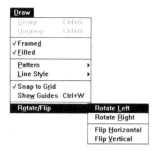

3. Click the type of effect you want. To help you visualize what happens, the following illustration shows you how the orientation of an object changes:

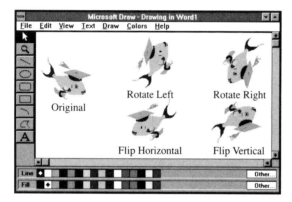

At the very least, you can have some fun trying out different effects—for example, by rotating multiple copies of a single object. On a more practical level, if you've ever drawn a valentine, a butterfly, or a pair of scissors, you know how difficult it is to make one side of a drawing mirror the other side exactly. With the Rotate/Flip command, it's no problem:

1. Draw half of the image and copy it to the Clipboard.

2. Paste the image back into your drawing.

3. Choose Rotate/Flip from the Draw menu and flip the copy vertically or horizontally, as necessary.

4. Select the copy and move it alongside the original half to create a mirror image.

Grouping Objects

As you add more and more objects to a drawing, you'll sometimes find it helpful to group related objects so that you can move, copy, and resize them as a single item. To do this,

1. Choose the Arrow tool and select all the objects you want to group. (Hold down Shift to select a sequence of objects, or drag to enclose objects in a selection rectangle.)

2. Choose the Group command from the Draw menu.

After you group a set of objects, Draw replaces the resize handles around each object with a set of four new resize handles set at the corners of an invisible rectangle around the group. You can now use the new resize handles to change the size or shape of the group. To move the grouped objects, point to an object and drag as usual with the mouse.

If you need to edit one of the grouped objects later on,

1. Select the grouped objects.

2. Ungroup the objects by choosing Ungroup from the Draw menu.

MOVING TO THE WORD PROCESSOR

When your drawing is complete and you're ready to embed it in a word processed document, do either of the following:

■ Choose Update from the File menu and then choose Exit And Return To *document name.*

■ Choose Exit And Return To *document name* from the File menu. In this case, Draw displays the message below, which asks whether you want to update the word processed document. Click Yes to embed the image and return to the document.

Whichever method you use, Works inserts the drawing wherever the insertion point was located in the word processed document at the time you started Draw.

If, when you embed the drawing, you find that your sense of scale was a little off and the drawing is not the size you expected, do either of the following:

■ Return to the drawing as described in the next section, and resize the image.

■ Choose Picture from the Format menu in the Word Processor. When you see the following dialog box, change the percentages to scale your drawing to a more suitable size. Unless you don't mind changing the proportions in your drawing, change the height and width of the picture equally.

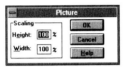

Once the drawing is in your word processed document, Works treats it as if it were a single new paragraph, so you can fine-tune its alignment and spacing above or below with the Format commands or the Toolbar.

RETURNING TO DRAW

If you find that your embedded drawing is not quite right, you can return to Draw from the Word Processor and edit the drawing whenever you want. Simply double-click on the drawing in the word processed document.

CHAPTER 6

Spreadsheet Basics

If the Word Processor is where you turn your imagination loose, the Spreadsheet is where you analyze and experiment with financial alternatives. The Spreadsheet is also your springboard into the Works charting module—Chapter 7 tells you how to turn spreadsheet data into any of several types of charts. And as mentioned in Chapter 10, the Spreadsheet is a place where you can create simple tables to copy into a word processed document.

Charts and tables are added benefits, however. The real job of any spreadsheet program lies in helping you organize and analyze numbers. In this chapter, you'll see how to

- Create and edit a spreadsheet
- Use formulas and predefined *functions* to make Works do your arithmetic for you
- Name groups of data for easy reference
- Find, sort, and protect your information
- Use formatting to make your spreadsheet look its best
- Preview and print a spreadsheet

STARTING THE SPREADSHEET

You can start the Spreadsheet in either of the following ways:

- Click the Spreadsheet button in either the Startup or the Create New File dialog box
- Choose a previously created spreadsheet (with the extension WKS) from the Open Existing File dialog box

The Spreadsheet Screen

If you start a new spreadsheet, your first view of the program looks like the screen on the next page, in which a few key items are labeled.

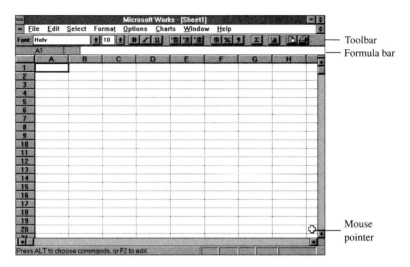

This illustration shows the grid of cells in which you enter text, data, and formulas. Both the application and document windows are maximized to take full advantage of onscreen space. Above the grid are two important features:

- The *Toolbar,* as in other Works applications, responds to the mouse to give you fast access to common procedures.

- The *formula bar* gives you a one-line "scratchpad" for viewing and editing spreadsheet entries. Although the cells below the formula bar show the actual layout and contents of your spreadsheet, you enter or edit information in the formula bar.

CELLS AND CELL REFERENCES

NOTE: *If computers or spreadsheets are new to you, the background information in this section will help you settle in and begin to feel at home. If you already know about cell references and cell ranges, skip ahead to "Creating a Spreadsheet."*

Chapter 2 described a spreadsheet as a grid of cells that form an on-screen version of a ledger sheet. But what exactly is a cell? Essentially, it's a pigeonhole into which you can type whatever information you want. In many ways, a cell is comparable to one of the postal boxes lining the wall at your post office. Just as a postal box can hold different types of mail—bills, magazines, or letters—a spreadsheet cell can hold different types of information (some of which are shown in Figure 6-1).

- Text, such as the words *Amount paid* or *Balance forward*
- Numeric values, such as *$1009.50*
- Formulas, such as *=Principal∗Interest*
- Dates and times, such as *8/11/92* and *12:00 AM*

Every time you open a spreadsheet in Works, you open a sheet of 4,194,304 cells arranged in 16,384 rows and 256 columns. Spreadsheet rows are numbered sequentially, from 1 through 16384. Columns are identified by letter: A, B, C, and so on. Because the alphabet contains only 26 letters, columns 27 through 256 are labeled AA through AZ, followed by BA through BZ, and so on through column IV.

Referring to Cells

Because each cell can hold one entry, a spreadsheet can theoretically contain more than four million separate entries. To refer to specific cells among the many potential locations for your data, you use ''addresses'' called *cell references.* A cell reference is made up of the letter that designates the column and the number that designates the row in which the cell appears—for example, A1 for the cell in column A, row 1; B1 for the cell in column B, row 1; and C100 for the cell in column C, row 100.

As you work on a spreadsheet, you move a thick-bordered *highlight* from cell to cell. The highlight always surrounds the *current cell,* the one you're working in. In Figure 6-1, for example, the highlight is on cell D9. Works always displays the address of the current cell at the top left of the screen, just above your work area.

Address of
current cell

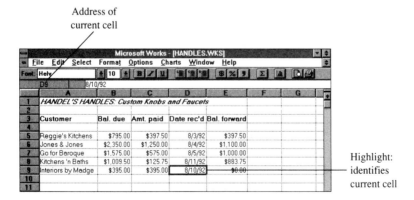

Highlight:
identifies
current cell

FIGURE 6-1. *The current cell is highlighted. Its location and contents are displayed in the formula bar.*

Selecting Cells

When you work with a spreadsheet, you *select* cells to

■ Show where you want your typing to appear

■ Point to a spreadsheet entry you want to work on

Because Works is a Windows program and Windows programs are mouse-oriented, you can cruise effortlessly from cell to cell with a few simple mouse techniques:

■ If you can see the cell you want to highlight, point to it and click.

■ If you can't see the cell you want, click the scroll bars until the cell comes into view. Then, point to it and click.

Often, especially during data entry, you'll find the keyboard as convenient as the mouse (or more so) for moving around in a spreadsheet. The following table lists keys you can use:

Key or Combination	Moves the Highlight
Left or Right arrow key	Left or right one column
Up or Down arrow key	Up or down one row
Home	To the first cell in the row
End	To the last column that contains data or formatting
Ctrl-Home	To the first cell in the spreadsheet (cell A1)
Ctrl-End	To the cell in the last row of the last column that contains data or formatting
PgUp or PgDn	Up or down one window (screenful)
Ctrl-PgUp or Ctrl-PgDn	Left or right one window (screenful)

Cell Ranges

Spreadsheets often contain sets of related data, such as item names, prices, amounts sold, or sales figures by item. You can work with any such set of cells as a *range,* a rectangular block of two or more cells. To refer to a range, you use a colon (:) to separate the first (top left) and last (bottom right) cell references. So, for example, a range including cells A4 through B9 would be referenced as A4:B9.

Why would you want to lump cells as a range? Perhaps to copy the contents of all the cells, to apply formatting (such as boldfacing) to them, or to include them in a total or some other formula. To make your work easier, you might even want to assign the cells a *range name,* a descriptive reference to all the cells in the range. (More on naming ranges later in this chapter.) As you work with spreadsheets, you'll find yourself working with ranges more often than not.

Selecting ranges

When you select an individual cell, a border appears around it. When you select a range of cells, the Spreadsheet *extends* the highlight, changing the background color of the selected cells:

Currently selected
range of cells

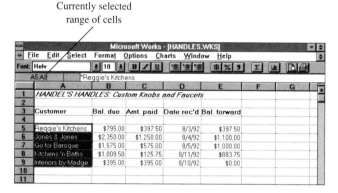

As with individual cells, ranges are easiest to select with the mouse:

1. Point to the first cell in the range. Any corner will do, although the cell at the top left will probably seem most "correct."

2. Drag the mouse until the highlight covers all the cells you want to select. If you overshoot, drag up or back to shrink the highlight. When you're satisfied, release the mouse button.

To "deselect" a range, click in any cell.

To use the keyboard for selecting a range,

1. Press F8 to turn on the Spreadsheet's *extend selection* mode.

2. Use the direction keys, such as the Down arrow key or the End key, to extend the highlight.

To turn off extend selection mode, press Esc.

You can also use the key combinations in the table on the next page to select a range of cells. As with the mouse technique for selecting ranges, these combinations do not turn on extend selection mode. (Left, Right, Up, and Down refer to the arrow keys.)

NOTE: *When you use these key combinations, Works considers a range to be any contiguous set of cells separated from other sets by one or more blank cells. With a little experimentation, you'll quickly see how these key combinations can be handy.*

Key Combination	Extends the Highlight
Shift-F8	Over an entire column
Ctrl-F8	Over an entire row
Shift-Home	To the beginning of a row
Shift-Arrow key	Left, right, up, or down one cell
Ctrl-Shift-Left	Left to the first cell in a range
Ctrl-Shift-Right	Right to the last cell in a range
Ctrl-Shift-Up	Up to the first cell in a range
Ctrl-Shift-Down	Down to the last cell in a range

CREATING A SPREADSHEET

You create a spreadsheet by selecting cells (one by one) and typing information into them. As you type, the Spreadsheet displays the entry in the formula bar. The basic steps for entering information are the following:

1. Move the highlight to the cell you want.

2. Type the data for that cell. To type numbers, use either the top row of keys on the keyboard or (after pressing Num Lock) the numeric keypad on the side.

3. Move the entry from the formula bar to its home in the current cell. Do this in either of the following ways:

   □ Click another cell or use the direction keys. Either method stores the entry and moves the highlight to another cell.

   □ Press Enter or click the Enter box (the one with a checkmark just to the left of the formula bar). Either method stores the entry but keeps the highlight in the same cell. Note that the Enter box and the Cancel box (the one with the ×) appear only after you begin to type data in the formula bar.

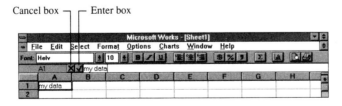

NOTE: *When you type a* text *entry that overflows the current cell, the Spreadsheet displays the complete text if the cell to the right is empty. If the adjoining cell is not empty, the Spreadsheet displays (and prints) only the part that fits into the cell. To display more of the text, widen the cell as described under "Changing Column Widths."*

Formatting Numbers

Typically, most entries in a spreadsheet are numeric, and Works gives you a choice of formats you can apply either before or after you type the numbers themselves. To apply number formats,

1. Select the cells you want to format.

2. Use the Toolbar or the Format menu to apply the format of your choice.

Using the Toolbar, you can quickly apply the Currency, Percent, and Comma (separator) formats, demonstrated here:

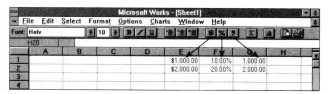

If you use the Format menu, you have a greater number of choices:

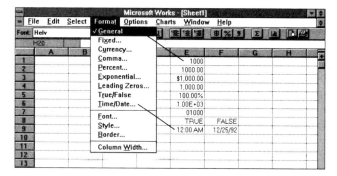

Formatting numbers is simple, but bear in mind this warning: You apply the formatting to the cells themselves, not merely to the values in them. Thus, if you delete a cell entry, you delete the number but not the formatting. To eliminate special formatting, select the cells and choose General from the Format menu.

Also, be aware that the displayed value in a cell (as formatted) might not match the actual value. In calculations, Works uses the actual value (which will appear in the formula bar), not the displayed value in the cell (which might be rounded or truncated).

The following list describes each of the number formats:

■ General, the default format, displays numbers as integers (whole numbers) or as decimal fractions with up to nine decimal places. A number too long for its cell is displayed in exponential form.

■ Fixed format displays numbers rounded to a specified number of decimal places. Choosing Fixed produces this dialog box:

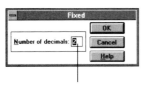

Type the number of decimal
places and click OK.

■ Currency formats numbers as currency values. Like Fixed and other number formats, the Currency option produces a dialog box that asks you to specify the number of decimals.

■ Comma inserts comma separators in large numbers. Again, you are asked to specify the number of decimals.

■ Percent formats numbers as percents. This format, too, asks for the number of decimals you want. When you type values into cells formatted for displaying percents, type the decimal *equivalent* of the percent: The Spreadsheet multiplies the value by 100. Thus, *90* becomes 9000.00%, whereas *.9* becomes 90.00%.

■ Exponential displays numbers in scientific notation (powers of 10). For example, 1200 is displayed as 1.20E+03, for 1.20 times 10 to the third power.

■ Leading Zeros adds as many zeros as necessary to the left of a number to fill out the number of digits you specify in this dialog box:

For example, specifying six digits and typing *1000* would produce 001000. Leading Zeros displays whole numbers only; it rounds fractions up or down to the next whole number.

■ True/False displays *TRUE* if a cell with this formatting contains any value other than 0, *FALSE* if the cell contains 0.

■ Time/Date formats numbers as times or dates. When you choose Time/Date, you see this dialog box:

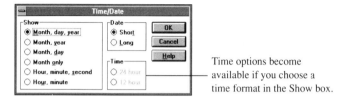

Time options become
available if you choose a
time format in the Show box.

Click a button in the Show box to choose the type of time or date you want. For a date, you can choose either a Short (12/25/92) or a Long (December 25, 1992) form in the Date box. To format time, you can choose a 24-hour (18:30) or 12-hour (06:30 PM) form in the Time box.

Entering Numbers as Text

Text is any character or group of characters that can't be used in calculations. In scanning a spreadsheet, you'll notice that Works aligns text at the left edge of the cell unless you specify otherwise, but it aligns numeric values to the right. Text is also preceded by a double quotation mark (") when it is displayed in the formula bar, even though the quotation mark does not appear in the cells or on your printed copies.

To enter a number (such as 1020), a date, or a time as text rather than as a numeric value, type a double quotation mark before typing the entry.

NOTE: *The Spreadsheet normally stores dates and times as serial numbers that can be displayed in any of several ways and can be added or subtracted to calculate elapsed intervals. Turn dates and times into text only if you do not want these capabilities.*

Using the Fill Commands

When you're building a spreadsheet, three commands on the Edit menu can save you time by filling in a series of cells with data or formulas:

■ The Fill Right and Fill Down commands copy a cell entry into adjoining cells, as shown on the next page.

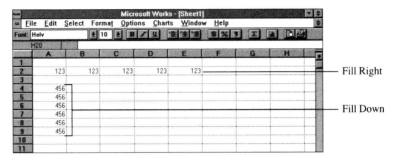

- The Fill Series command takes a starting number or date and fills adjoining cells (either below or to the right) with consecutive numbers or dates in a series:

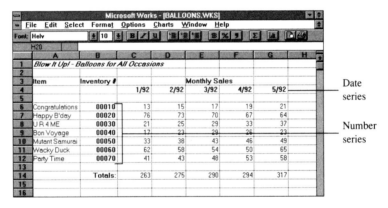

To use the Fill Right or Fill Down command,

1. Highlight the first cell in the series and type the entry you want adjoining cells to contain. Press Enter.

2. Select the cells you want to fill, starting with the cell containing the entry to be duplicated.

3. Choose Fill Right or Fill Down from the Edit menu.

As soon as you choose the command, Works fills the selected cells with copies of the original entry. (If you fill cells with formulas, Works automatically adjusts their cell references for you.)

To use the Fill Series command,

1. Highlight the first cell in the series and type a number or a date. If you type a date, use one of these forms: December; December 92; 12/92; 12/25/92; or December 25, 1992.

2. Select the cells you want to fill, beginning with the cell that contains the first entry.

3. Choose Fill Series from the Edit menu. When you do, the following dialog box appears. Click OK after you make any necessary changes:

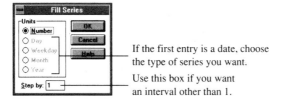

If the first entry is a date, choose the type of series you want.

Use this box if you want an interval other than 1.

CREATING FORMULAS

By taking advantage of your computer's mathematical ability, you can have the Spreadsheet perform the repetitive work of calculating results based on the data in your spreadsheet. The program can calculate with any figures you tell it to use, and because it can recalculate and give you new results automatically, you can be sure that your spreadsheet is always accurate, even if you make a small change in one of several hundred values.

Works can use either of two types of formulas: those you create yourself, and those that rely on prewritten instructions built into Works as functions. When you create formulas of your own, you put together the cell references, numbers, and arithmetic symbols needed to calculate the result you want. When you use built-in functions, you enter values or cell references into a predesigned formula. When necessary, you can also use functions as parts of larger formulas.

Entering a Formula

When you want to create a formula or use a built-in function,

1. Highlight the cell in which you want to enter the formula or function.

2. Type an equal sign (=). This is important. If you forget, the Spreadsheet won't calculate a result for you.

3. Type the formula. The Spreadsheet displays the characters you type in the formula bar, and a blinking *insertion point* shows where the next character or cell reference will appear.

4. Press Enter or click the Enter button (the one with the checkmark) on the formula bar.

Simple as these steps sound, Spreadsheet formulas can become complex, especially if you want a single calculation to involve several operations. The Spreadsheet does offer a number of tools to help you build formulas. These are described in the following sections. A list of built-in functions appears in Appendix B.

The Autosum Button

Because many spreadsheet calculations rely on totals, Works offers a quick method of totaling a row or column of figures—the Autosum button on the Toolbar:

Autosum button

To total figures with the Autosum button,

1. Highlight the cell in which you want a total to appear.

2. Click the Autosum button. The Spreadsheet automatically searches up and to the left to find a column or row of figures to total and displays the cell references in the formula bar in this form: *=SUM(D1:D3)*.

   If the cell references are not the ones you intended or if you see *=SUM()* in the formula bar (meaning that the Spreadsheet could not find a valid group of figures to total), type the correct cell references or highlight the cells you want to total.

3. Click the Autosum button again, press Enter, or click the Enter box in the formula bar.

NOTE: *You can double-click the Autosum button to produce a total immediately. If you do this, check the formula beforehand to be sure the cell references are correct.*

Cell References in Formulas

When you create formulas, you can type numbers or you can include cell references. Cell references are variables: The Spreadsheet uses whatever value is in each cell you reference. Thus, the formula *=A1+B1* yields the sum of the values in cells A1 and B1.

To include a cell reference in a formula, do either of the following:

■ Type the reference—for example *A1* for a single cell or *A1:A6* for a cell range.

■ Highlight the cell or cells you want in the formula. The Spreadsheet displays the cell reference in the formula bar, and it becomes a part of the formula (or function) as soon as you type an operator, such as the plus sign, or as soon as you end the formula by pressing the Enter key or clicking the Enter box in the formula bar.

You can substitute range names for cell references in both formulas and functions. Later in this chapter, the section titled ''Naming Ranges'' tells you how to assign names to cell ranges.

Controlling Cell References

By default, the Spreadsheet uses *relative cell references,* which point to cells a relative distance away from the current cell. If, as described under ''Editing a Spreadsheet,'' you move or copy a formula containing relative cell references, the Spreadsheet automatically adjusts the references, changing the formula so that it refers to cells in the same positions, *relative to* the formula's new location. Thus a formula in A3 that finds the difference of the two cells above it (*A1–A2*) changes, by default, when moved to D3 so that it finds the difference of the same two cells in column D (*D1–D2*).

You can override the relative adjustments to cell addresses in formulas by using either *absolute* or *mixed* references. Absolute references always point to the same cell, no matter where you move the formula. Mixed references are those in which one part of the cell reference, either row or column, is absolute and the other part is relative.

To create an absolute reference, do either of the following:

■ Type a dollar sign in front of both the column and row designations in the cell reference—for example, *A1.*

■ Highlight the cell or cells that are to be absolute references and then press F4 until a dollar sign appears in front of both the column and row designations in the formula bar.

To create a mixed reference, do either of the following:

■ Type a dollar sign in front of the part of the address that you want to be absolute—for example, *A$1* if the column can be relative but the row must always be row 1.

■ Highlight the cell or cells and press F4 until a dollar sign appears in front of the absolute part of the address.

For additional explanations of relative, absolute, and mixed references, open the Spreadsheet's Help window and use the Search command to find entries on these types of cell references.

Operators

In a formula, operators control the type of calculation the Spreadsheet will perform. The following table lists valid Spreadsheet operators, with examples showing how they can be used. (Logical evaluations use sample range names for clarity.)

Operator	Example
+ (addition)	2+2 or A1+B1
− (subtraction)	5−3 or A1−B1
+ (positive)	+2
− (negative)	−2
* (multiplication)	2*2 or A1*B1
/ (division)	12/6 or A1/B1
^ (exponentiation)	10^2
= (equal to)	2=2 or A1=B1
<> (not equal to)	2<>3 or A1<>B1
< (less than)	2<3 or A1<B1
> (greater than)	2>1 or A1>B1
<= (less than or equal to)	2<=3 or A1<=B1
>= (greater than or equal to)	2>=1 or A1>=B1
~ (NOT)	Profits~Losses
| (OR)	Salaries | Commissions
& (AND)	Salaries&Benefits

Controlling the Order of Evaluation

Formulas are sometimes much more complex than a simple 2+2 or A1+B1. Many combine various types of calculations, like this:

2+3*4/5^6

In principle, such a formula can be calculated in any of several ways. Working from left to right, you would add 2 and 3, multiply the result (5) by 4, divide the product (20) by 5, and then raise that result (4) to the sixth power to get 4096. The Spreadsheet, however, follows a *standard order of evaluation,* in which it scans a formula and evaluates operators in the order shown on the next page.

Order of evaluation	Operator
First	− (negative) and + (positive)
Second	^
Third	* and /
Fourth	+ (addition) and − (subtraction)
Fifth	= <> < > <= >=
Sixth	~
Seventh	| and &

Following this order of evaluation, the formula 2+3*4/5^6 produces 2.00768: First, 5^6 yields 15625; second, 3*4 is divided by 15625, which is 0.00768; third, that result is added to 2, which produces 2.00768, vastly different from 4096.

To control the order in which the Spreadsheet performs its calculations, you can enclose portions of the formula in sets of parentheses (). When-ever it encounters parentheses in a formula, the Spreadsheet evaluates the portion within the parentheses before resorting to its standard order of evaluation. If, as in the preceding example, you want to control mul-tiple operations, you can nest sets of parentheses, one inside the other. The Spreadsheet then calculates outward, from the innermost set of pa-rentheses. For example, the following sets of parentheses would override the standard order of evaluation to produce 4096:

`((2+3)*4/5)^6.`

Viewing Formulas and Functions

Normally, the Spreadsheet displays the results of your formulas, rather than the formulas themselves. If you're working on an elaborate spread-sheet, you'll probably want to view (or review) your formulas to resolve problems or to check for accuracy. To do this, turn on the Show For-mulas option on the Options menu.

A checkmark appears next to the option when it is turned on, and your spreadsheet columns automatically widen to display the formulas (and functions) you've entered. Scroll as necessary to view other parts of the spreadsheet.

EDITING A SPREADSHEET

Spreadsheets do not always spring flawlessly into being. In fact, one tre-mendous value of spreadsheets is the ease with which you can test the results produced by changing conditions. To edit entries—text, data, or formulas—as you type, you can simply backspace over an error.

Replacing Entries

If you want to replace a completed entry,

1. Highlight the cell.

2. Type the new entry, and press Enter or click the Enter box.

If you're typing a replacement but want to restore the previous entry, click the Cancel box (marked with an ×) or press Esc.

Editing Entries

If you want to edit a completed entry,

1. Highlight the cell; then, press F2 to request Edit mode, or point and click in the formula bar to position the insertion point at the place you want to edit.

2. To insert characters to the left of the insertion point, simply type. To delete characters to the right of the insertion point, press the Del key.

To replace or delete a block of characters in the current cell,

1. Select the characters: Drag with the mouse, or hold down the Shift key and press the Right or Left arrow key.

2. Replace highlighted characters simply by typing what you want in their stead. (You can replace cell references either by typing or by highlighting the cells you want.) Delete highlighted characters by pressing the Del key.

Changing Column Widths

When you open a new spreadsheet, Works sets each column to a width of 10 characters. You can change the column width whenever you want, however, either before or after you've entered data. You might, for instance, want to narrow a column to a few characters if it contains only single-digit or double-digit percents. At the other extreme, you'll find that typing large numbers sometimes causes the Spreadsheet to display a series of number signs (#########) or a number in exponential notation, instead of the digits you type. This happens because the cell is not wide enough for the entire number.

To change the width of a spreadsheet column, use the mouse or the Column Width command on the Format menu:

- With the mouse, point to the right boundary between columns at the top of the spreadsheet grid:

Mouse pointer in position to
change width of column C

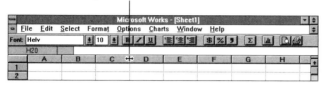

Hold down the left button and drag to the left or right. As you drag, a dotted vertical line follows the mouse pointer. Release the mouse button when the column has the width you want.

- For more precise control, open the Format menu, choose the Column Width command, and change the width in the resulting dialog box:

   Type the width you prefer, in
characters, and then click OK.

Inserting and Deleting Rows and Columns

Spreadsheets eventually become nicely organized sets of headings and data, but the layout sometimes requires a little work during the building process. You might, for instance, leave several blank rows for headings and later find you didn't need them after all. Or you might find that you left no room for a subtotal you now find necessary. In either case, you can add or delete as many rows or columns as you want.

Hiding Columns, Collapsing Spreadsheets

You can make a column disappear by narrowing its width to 0. This is a useful way to "collapse" a spreadsheet when you want to view nonadjacent columns. To make a hidden column visible again, choose the Go To command (described later) and type a cell reference, such as *G1*, within the hidden column. Although the highlight might seem to disappear, don't stop. Immediately choose the Column Width command and type a nonzero width. Click OK, and the hidden column will reappear.

To insert a row or column,

1. Highlight the row above which you want the new row, or highlight the column to the left of which you want the new column. To do this, click the row number or the column letter. (Selecting the entire row or column isn't necessary, but it speeds the process.)

2. Choose the Insert Row/Column command from the Edit menu.

As soon as you choose the command, the new row or column appears in the spreadsheet and the existing rows or columns are renumbered to account for the new one. If you select a cell instead of an entire row or column, choosing the Insert Row/Column command produces the following dialog box:

Click the type of insert you want, and then click OK.

To delete a row or column, follow the same procedure but choose the Delete Row/Column command from the Edit menu. Note, however, that although insertions add a row or column above or to the left of the selection, deletions remove the actual row or column you've highlighted.

REORGANIZING A SPREADSHEET

One of the advantages of using an electronic spreadsheet lies in the ease with which you can make changes—without the mess of erasing or of cutting pages apart and pasting them back together. In editing a spreadsheet, you might want to insert, move, cut, or copy its contents. Several of these maneuvers rely on that special, set-aside portion of your computer's memory known as the Clipboard.

The Clipboard is a temporary way station for data you cut (remove) or copy (duplicate) with the Cut and Copy commands on the Edit menu. You can freely reuse the contents of the Clipboard until you replace it with newly cut or copied information. To retrieve the contents of the Clipboard, use the Paste or Paste Special commands, also on the Edit menu. Both commands reinsert cut or copied information into the same or a different spreadsheet.

Deleting Information

You can delete cell contents with either of two commands:

■ Clear, which eliminates the contents of selected cells

■ Cut, which deletes the contents of selected cells but saves the information on the Clipboard

To delete information,

1. Highlight the cell or cells.

2. Do one of the following:

    □ Choose Clear from the Edit menu to erase the cell contents.

    □ Choose Cut from the Edit menu (or press Ctrl-X) to cut the cell contents to the Clipboard.

NOTE: *If you're experimenting with a spreadsheet, consider using Cut rather than Clear for deletions. If you do so, you'll be able to "undo" an inadvertent deletion with the Paste command, described below.*

Copying Information

When you copy information, you leave the original in the spreadsheet and place a duplicate on the Clipboard. After the information is on the Clipboard, you can insert it as described in the next section.

To copy cell contents, either data or formulas,

1. Highlight the cells whose contents you want to copy.

2. Choose the Copy command from the Edit menu or press Ctrl-C.

Inserting Cell Contents

To insert new data or formulas in a spreadsheet, you simply highlight a cell and type the new entry. The new entry replaces the former contents of the cell. To insert information from the Clipboard:

1. Highlight the first (top left-hand) cell that will receive the incoming information.

2. Do one of the following to insert the Clipboard contents:

    □ Choose Paste from the Edit menu or press Ctrl-V.

    □ Choose Paste Special from the Edit menu.

Both the Paste and Paste Special commands insert the contents of the Clipboard, filling as many cells as needed, going down and to the right of the highlighted cell. If any cells in the receiving range contain information, their contents will be overwritten or modified by the corresponding Clipboard contents.

Paste vs. Paste Special

The Paste and Paste Special commands give you several different ways to insert the contents of the Clipboard:

■ Paste inserts both data and formulas; it always overwrites existing cell contents. When inserting a formula, the Spreadsheet automatically adjusts cell references to suit their new location.

■ The Paste Special command gives you several options, listed in its dialog box:

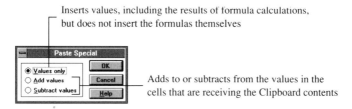

Inserts values, including the results of formula calculations, but does not insert the formulas themselves

Adds to or subtracts from the values in the cells that are receiving the Clipboard contents

NOTE: *Works is very good at adjusting cell references when you move or copy formulas, but it's always smart to verify the references yourself, especially if your formulas contain absolute or mixed references.*

FORMATTING A SPREADSHEET

Content aside, a spreadsheet can gain considerable impact and clarity from careful formatting. Aside from number formats, described earlier in this chapter, you can control fonts (typefaces), font sizes, and font styles. Your choice of font and font size helps you determine the number of columns on the screen or the amount of data on the printed page. To emphasize important portions of your spreadsheet, you can apply font styles to certain cells or draw borders around cells and their contents.

The following sections briefly describe how to apply formatting to a spreadsheet. If you need additional background information, refer to the heading "Formatting" in Chapter 4.

Fonts and Font Sizes

When you apply a particular font or size to a spreadsheet, you affect the entire document. In this respect, the Spreadsheet is unlike the Word Processor, which allows you to combine different fonts and sizes within a document. Otherwise, however, the Spreadsheet is very similar to both the Word Processor and the Database.

- The fonts and sizes available to you are determined by the make and model of printer you use.

- You can choose fonts and font sizes either with the Toolbar or with the Font command on the Format menu.

If you use the Toolbar,

- Click the down arrow to the right of the Font list box to see a list of available fonts. Click the font of your choice.

- Click the down arrow to the right of the size box to see a list of available sizes for the font you've chosen. Click the size you want.

Font ⌐ Font size

If you choose the Font command on the Format menu, indicate the font and size you want in the resulting dialog box:

Choose a font   Choose a size for
from this list.   the font you chose.

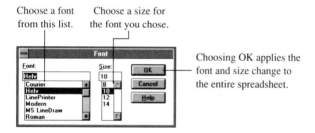

Choosing OK applies the font and size change to the entire spreadsheet.

Font Styles

Font styles comprise qualities such as boldfacing and italics. With the Toolbar, you can apply any combination of three font styles:

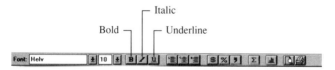

⌐ Italic

Bold ⌐ ⌐ Underline

Unlike fonts and sizes, which affect the entire spreadsheet, font styles affect selected cells. To apply any or all of these styles:

1. Highlight the cells whose contents you want to format.

2. Click the button or buttons on the Toolbar that apply the styles.

You can also apply font styles with the Style command on the Format menu. When you choose this command, you see the dialog box below. As is often the case in Works, the dialog box offers more choices than the Toolbar does.

■ Alignment refers to the alignment of cell contents within the cell. Click the type of alignment you want. General, the default, aligns text to the left and numbers to the right.

■ Styles offers the same choices as the Toolbar. Click the style or styles you want.

■ Locked is a special option that locks cell contents so that they can be viewed but not changed. Click the Locked box when you want to protect valuable or sensitive data. A warning, however: Locked alone *does not* apply protection. You must also choose the Protect Data command from the Options menu. Only when both Locked and Protect Data are turned on is your data safe from inadvertent change. To turn protection off entirely, deselect both options.

Borders

The Borders command, available only through the Format menu, draws a border around selected cells. To add a border to your spreadsheet,

1. Select the cells whose contents you want bordered.

2. Choose the Borders command. The following dialog box appears:

Click the appropriate box to add a full (outline) border or a partial border along the top, bottom, left, or right edge (or some combination) of the selected cell or cells.

The Spreadsheet draws a border along the boundaries of the cell. If you widen or narrow the cell, the border changes to fit.

Naming Ranges

Range names represent one of the most useful ''nonessential'' features of the Works Spreadsheet. If you assign names to groups of cells, you can navigate quickly from one block of cells to another. Even better, you can use range names in place of cell references in your formulas to make the formulas far more descriptive than they would otherwise be to yourself and, especially, to others.

You can assign a name to any cell or group of cells you want. You can even overlap named ranges as shown below:

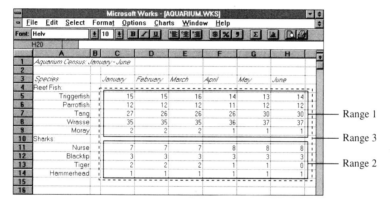

To assign a range name, do the following:

1. Highlight the cell or cells you want to name.

2. Choose the Range Name command from the Edit menu. The following dialog box appears:

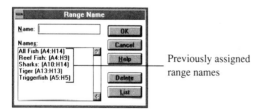

Previously assigned range names

3. Type the name you want and click OK.

Each time you assign a range name, the Spreadsheet adds the name to the list it displays in the Names portion of the Range Name dialog box. Notice that the dialog box also includes Delete and List buttons:

■ The Delete button deletes a range name. To use it, click the name you want to delete, click the Delete button, and then click the button marked Close. (When you delete range names, the Close button replaces the Cancel button in the dialog box above.)

■ The List button produces a list of range names and the cells they reference in your spreadsheet. If you're going to use the List button, first highlight a cell that is below or to the right of your data and formulas. After you choose the List button, the Spreadsheet displays a two-column list beginning in the cell you highlighted and extending down as many rows as you have range names. If any cells in that block contain data or formulas, the incoming list will overwrite (and destroy) their contents.

Locating Parts of a Spreadsheet

Whatever the size of your spreadsheet, you can find and highlight specific cells, cell ranges, and even data almost effortlessly with the Spreadsheet's Go To and Find commands, both on the Select menu.

Going To cells and cell ranges

The Go To command works perfectly well with cell references, but it's especially easy to use with range names. To use the command,

1. Press F5 or choose Go To from the Select menu. The following dialog box appears:

2. If you're using range names, choose the name from the list in the Names box or type the name in the Go To box. To go to an unnamed cell or group of cells, type the cell reference in the Go To box.

Avoiding Rocky Range Names

When naming ranges, try to avoid using numbers, cell references, or function names as range names. Names such as *1992*, *A1*, and *AVG*, for example, are ambiguous and can be misinterpreted if you try to include them in formulas. If you create such a name and need to use it in a formula, surround it with single quotation marks, as in this example: ='1992'/12.

As soon as you press Enter or click OK to carry out the command, the Spreadsheet jumps to, and highlights, the cell or range of cells you specified.

Finding specific information

To highlight a specific entry—text, number, or formula—in a spreadsheet, use the Find command:

1. Choose Find from the Select menu. The following dialog box appears:

2. Type the entry you seek (or a significant part of the entry) in the Find What box.

3. Click in the Look By box to tell the Spreadsheet how to scan for the entry: row by row, or column by column.

When you press Enter or click OK, the highlight jumps to the first occurrence of the entry you specified. If the same entry appears more than once in a spreadsheet, press F7 to repeat the search.

Sorting a Spreadsheet

If your spreadsheet contains columns of data, you might sometimes want to see your data arranged differently, in either ascending (0–9 or A–Z) or descending (9–0 or Z–A) order. To rearrange rows of data, you use the Sort Rows command:

1. Highlight the cells in the rows you want to sort. The Sort Rows command rearranges entire rows, but you might save time by highlighting a block of rows in a single column (especially if you select the primary sort column, explained below).

2. Choose Sort Rows from the Select menu and specify column letters and sort orders, as shown in the dialog box in Figure 6-2.

When you press Enter or click OK, the Spreadsheet immediately sorts the values in the specified columns, arranging them as you requested.

The 1st Column, 2nd Column, and 3rd Column boxes let you specify up to three columns of data to sort. The 1st Column produces a *primary* sort, in which the entries in that column are arranged in ascending or descending order. If duplicates appear in the first column, you can specify second and, if necessary, third columns to guide the Spreadsheet in arranging the duplicates. Figure 6-2 shows the effects of selecting three columns to sort.

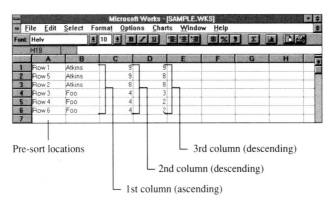

FIGURE 6-2. *The options chosen in the Sort Rows dialog box result in the rearrangement shown.*

PRINTING A SPREADSHEET

Printing from the Spreadsheet is remarkably similar to printing from the Word Processor. The following sections describe features of printing that are specific to the Spreadsheet. For details on headers, page orientation, and printing in general, refer to Chapter 4, beginning with the section "Defining Page Layouts."

Setting Up

To define the overall layout of your printed page, choose Page Setup & Margins from the File menu. The following dialog box appears:

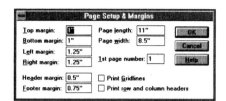

Define the margins, page size, and page numbering, as you do in the Word Processor. Two printing options are specific to the Spreadsheet:

- Click the Print Gridlines box if you want your printout to include gridlines, as they appear on the screen.

- Click the Print Row And Column Headers box if you want to include row numbers and column letters on your printout.

Printing Part of a Spreadsheet

If you choose to print gridlines and row and column headers, the printed grid will cover the entire page (except the margins) even if much of the page contains no data. You can print only a portion of the grid, however, with the Set Print Area command:

1. Highlight the cells you want to print.

2. Choose Set Print Area from the File menu.

These simple steps ensure that Works prints only the portion of the spreadsheet you want. Once you set the print area, however, it remains set to the same group of cells (for the current spreadsheet only), even if you move the highlight or enter new data. To reset the print area to the entire spreadsheet:

1. Highlight the entire spreadsheet by choosing All from the Select menu or by clicking the rectangular box above and to the left of the row and column headers.

Click here to highlight
the entire spreadsheet.

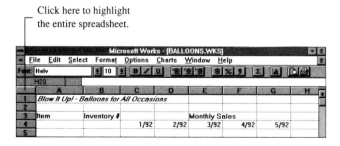

2. Choose the Set Print Area command again.

Previewing and Printing

Even before printing, you can see what your spreadsheet will look like. To preview a document, do one of the following:

■ Click the Print Preview button on the Toolbar:

Print Preview ─┐ ┌─ Print

■ Choose Print Preview from the File menu.

Either method produces a display like the one below. To see a close-up of your document, zoom in and out by clicking the Zoom buttons.

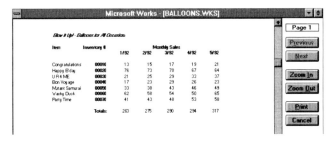

When you're satisfied with the look of your spreadsheet, you can send it to the printer in any of these ways:

■ Click the Print button (from Print Preview).

■ Click the Print button on the Toolbar.

■ Press Ctrl-P.

■ Choose Print from the File menu.

No matter how you initiate printing, Works displays this dialog box:

Click Pages and type the beginning and ending page numbers if you want to print part of a multiple-page document. Click Draft Quality Printing if you want a fast printout.

CHAPTER 7

Chart Basics

A chart of any type turns a set of numbers into a graphic that tells the viewer, at a glance, how those numbers are related to one another. With Works, a spreadsheet and a click of the mouse are all you need to create a basic bar chart, one that uses bars of different sizes to represent the values you want to show. You're not limited to bar charts, though. With a few more clicks, you can change the bars to lines, dots, or slices of a pie. To refine your chart, you can add titles and other descriptive text, format the text in a font and size you like, and even mix and match patterns or colors. When you're satisfied, you can print the chart or, through the magic of Windows and Works, *embed* a copy of the chart in a word processed document. (For embedded charts, refer to Chapter 10.)

This chapter tells you how to create all the different types of charts, as well as how to

■ Add titles, legends, and labels

■ Choose fonts, patterns, and colors

■ Adjust the horizontal and vertical axes

■ Name, duplicate, and delete charts

■ View and print charts

NOTE: *If you have a color monitor, Works normally displays the values on your charts in different colors. This is not a colorful book, however, and so patterns replace colors for the examples in this chapter. In other respects, however, what you see here should be what you get on your own system.*

CREATING A CHART

To create a chart, you start with a spreadsheet that contains the values you need. Most of the examples in this chapter are based on the sample spreadsheet in Figure 7-1.

Microsoft Works - [SELLSODA.WKS]

File Edit Select Format Options Charts Window Help

Font: Helv   10   B / U

H20

	A	B	C	D	E	F	G	H
1	MyCola Soda Sales: Jan - June 1992							
2								
3		January	February	March	April	May	June	
4	MyCola	3,241	2,482	1,836	1,922	2,587	2,694	
5	Sunny Citrus	2,673	2,416	2,012	1,787	1,974	2,368	
6	Hoot'n Root Beer	1,423	1,171	1,286	1,455	1,346	1,379	
7	Kiwi Treat	912	873	896	931	865	927	
8	Crackleberry	753	798	637	846	790	872	
9	Lime Supreme	1,864	2,233	2,165	2,257	2,670	3,121	
10								
11	Total	10,866	9,973	8,832	9,198	10,232	11,361	
12								

FIGURE 7-1. *A sample spreadsheet that shows unit sales by month.*

Selecting Values to Chart

In creating a chart, your first order of business is to highlight the portion of the spreadsheet that you want the chart to represent. Give some thought to your selection because the text and values you highlight determine how Works will lay out your chart.

A bar chart (or any other type except a pie chart), has two *axes,* one running horizontally, called the X-axis, and another running vertically, the Y-axis. When Works creates the chart, it uses the X-axis for *categories* of data and turns the Y-axis into a *scale* against which it plots the values you highlight. Of course, Works does not understand the meaning of your spreadsheet data, so it obeys the following rules in determining what to place on the X-axis and what values to plot against the Y-axis:

■ If you highlight more columns than rows, Works assumes that each column represents a category and each row contains values to be plotted. If it finds text in the first row of highlighted cells, Works uses the text as *category labels* in your chart, like this:

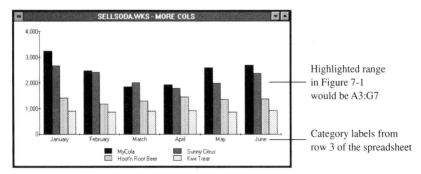

Highlighted range in Figure 7-1 would be A3:G7

Category labels from row 3 of the spreadsheet

■ If you highlight more rows than columns, Works assumes that each row represents a category and each column contains values to be plotted. If it finds text in the first column of highlighted cells, Works uses the text as category labels, like this:

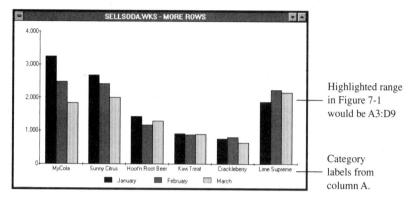

Highlighted range in Figure 7-1 would be A3:D9

Category labels from column A.

NOTE: *In dialog boxes and in Help topics, you'll see categories on the X-axis referred to as the* category (X) series. *Works can plot up to six sets of values on the Y-axis, so you'll find them called the first through sixth* value (Y) series.

The Chart Itself

After you highlight the text and values you want to chart, creating a chart is simple:

■ Click the Chart button on the Spreadsheet Toolbar:

Chart button

■ Or choose Create New Chart from the Charts menu.

Either of these options activates the charting module and takes you to a new application window. In the window, you see your data in the form of a bar chart like those illustrated earlier.

A bar chart is easily understood and widely used, but it's not always the best choice for your data, so the charting module gives you several other types from which to choose. As you work, you can transform your chart into a different chart type whenever you want.

Choosing a Chart Type

To choose a new chart type, you can use the charting-window Toolbar, as shown below, or you can pick a chart type from the Gallery menu.

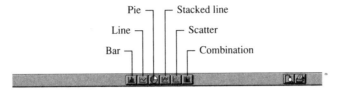

Whichever approach you take, a dialog box appears, such as the one in Figure 7-2. It shows pictures of four to six variations of the chart type you chose.

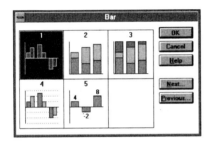

FIGURE 7-2. *The Bar dialog box lets you choose from among five variations of that basic chart type.*

To choose one of the variations, double-click the option, or highlight your choice and click OK.

The Next and Previous buttons appear at the right of the dialog box for each chart type:

■ Click Next to see the dialog box for the next chart type (as determined by the button order on the Toolbar).

■ Click Previous to see the dialog box for the previous chart type.

The following sections briefly describe the various chart types. The easiest way to see differences among them, however, is to experiment on your own screen.

Bar charts

Bar charts, as mentioned, show values as bars of varying length. In a standard bar chart of the kind Works creates by default, positive values appear above the X-axis, negative values below. The Bar dialog box also lets you create a standard bar chart with horizontal gridlines or with labels showing the actual values represented by the bars. These options help your viewer interpret the chart.

In addition to these variations, the Bar dialog box offers two types of stacked bar chart: Values in each category are stacked on top of one another and are either totalled or shown proportionally as segments of a bar representing 100 percent.

Line charts

Line charts show data values as markers connected by a line and are commonly used for showing trends over time:

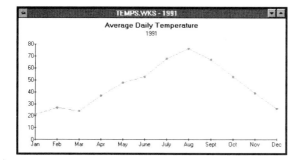

The Line dialog box offers six options. Most of the variations involve adding or omitting markers, lines, and horizontal or vertical gridlines. The sixth option, however, produces a *hi-lo-close chart* that connects the markers in each category with a vertical line. A hi-lo-close chart shows the difference between minimum and maximum values in a category, and a third (optional) value, typically a closing price or an average:

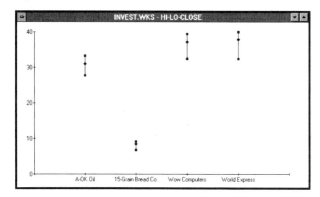

Pie charts

Pie charts, typical of the "how your tax dollar is spent" charts you see in newspapers and magazines, display a single set of values as individual slices of a pie, which represents 100 percent:

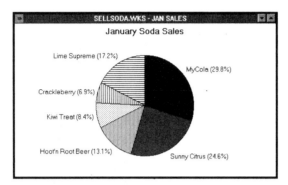

The pie chart dialog box offers six variations. The first four label the slices of a pie with combinations of category names and percents. The last two variations explode outward either the first or all slices of the pie.

NOTE: *If you create a pie chart, be sure not to highlight more than one set of values. Works charts only the first set of values in the selection, even if you highlight others.*

Stacked line charts

Similar to ordinary line charts, stacked line charts use markers and lines to connect values in each series. In addition, however, these charts stack the lines to show you the total for the values in each category. The following chart, for example, shows that sales for Sunny Citrus (the second line from the bottom) dropped from March to April, but total soda sales rose in the same period:

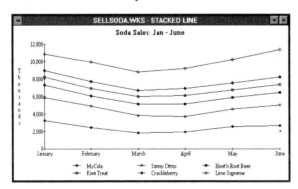

Notice that the markers and lines are stacked on top of one another and that the topmost markers represent the totals for each category.

When you create a stacked line chart, you can choose from four options. The default produces a standard stacked line chart. The remaining options add gridlines to the chart—horizontal, vertical, or both.

X-Y (scatter) charts

X-Y (scatter) charts are used to show how values are distributed—scattered against scales on both the X-axis and Y-axis. This type of chart is useful in determining whether, and how strongly, two sets of values are related. You would use such a chart for comparisons, such as test scores versus hours of study:

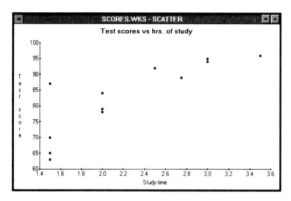

Unlike the other chart types, an X-Y chart cannot be created directly from a selected block of cells: You must specify the scales for both the X-axis and Y-axis. The following steps will create an X-Y chart:

1. In the Spreadsheet, highlight the data you want to use as the basis for the X-axis. The data must be numeric. Copy the values to the Clipboard with the Copy command on the Edit menu.

2. Still in the Spreadsheet, highlight the data you want to use as the basis for the Y-axis.

3. Click the Chart button on the Toolbar to create a standard bar chart showing your single set of values plotted against the Y-axis.

4. Now you're working in the charting window. Choose the Paste Series command from the Edit menu. When the following dialog box appears, click Category to paste the copied data into the chart as values for the X-axis of the chart.

5. Click the X-Y chart button on the Toolbar and, if you want, choose one of the chart options from the resulting dialog box.

NOTE: *Although some of the preceding steps might not be meaningful at this point, they do work. The remainder of this chapter and the charting module's Help menu should clarify matters.*

When you create an X-Y chart, you can choose among five variations that give you combinations of markers, lines, and gridlines. A sixth option gives you both a logarithmic scale and horizontal gridlines.

Combination charts

Combination charts merge chart types by using combinations of lines, bars, and markers to plot separate value series, like this:

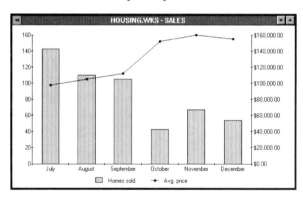

When you create a combination chart, you can choose from among four combinations of bars, lines, and scaling on one or two vertical axes.

FORMATTING A CHART

After you create a chart, you can enhance it with explanatory text and labels, choose the font and font size best suited to it, and experiment with patterns and colors as much as you want. To help make the chart more useful, you can adjust the scaling on either axis. You can also add a right vertical axis, even if the chart-type dialog box doesn't include an option with this feature.

Adding Titles

Titles are as important to charts as they are to books—more so, in fact, because by itself, labeling the axes or pie slices can seldom place a chart completely in perspective. To add titles and other text to a chart, choose the Titles command from the charting module's Edit menu. In the resulting dialog box, notice that Works lumps several types of text under the Titles command:

- Chart Title—type the main title for your chart.

- Subtitle—type a secondary title for your chart.

- Horizontal (X) Axis—type a description of the chart's categories.

- Vertical (Y) Axis—type a description of the chart's vertical axis.

- Right Vertical Axis—type a description of the chart's second (right) vertical axis, if any.

The following chart shows a labeled example of each kind of title:

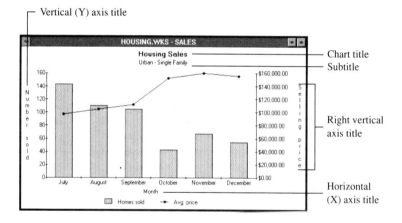

Adding Legends

Legends in charts are like legends on maps and in atlases. In a chart, legends identify the colors, patterns, or markers used for each value series, as shown on the next page.

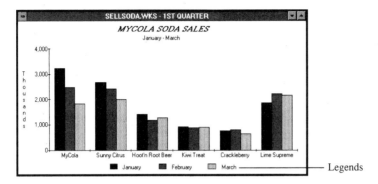

Legends

When you create a chart, Works automatically creates legends if it finds text either above or to the left of the values being charted. As you work with a chart, you can create, change, or delete legends easily. To accomplish any of these tasks, first choose the Legend command from the Edit menu. The following dialog box appears:

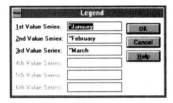

For each value series in your chart, Works displays *XX Value Series* in dark characters. If it created legends when it created the chart, the legends are displayed in the box to the right of each value series.

■ To create a legend, either type the legend text in the appropriate series box or type the reference of a cell that contains the text you want.

■ To delete a legend, double-click or drag to highlight the text or cell reference, and press the Del key.

■ To edit a legend, position the insertion point with the direction keys or mouse; type to insert new characters, or press Del to delete characters.

Including Data Labels

Several options in the chart-type dialog boxes add data labels to charts, among them option 5 in the Bar dialog box (Figure 7-2) and options 2, 3, and 4 in the Pie dialog box. You're not limited to these options, however. After you've created a chart, you can use the Data Labels command to label whatever data points you want. The labels you use can be either the actual values of the data or some other text or value that you provide. The following bar chart, for example, shows percents (rounded to the nearest whole number) used as data labels:

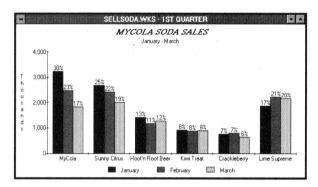

NOTE: *Unlike legends, labels you add to a chart must already exist on the spreadsheet. To create new labels, you must enter the text or values you want into cells on the spreadsheet.*

Adding data labels to bar and line charts

To add data labels to a bar or line chart, choose the Data Labels command on the Edit menu. This dialog box appears:

- To label data points with their actual values, click the Use Series Data box.

- To label data points with other text or values,

  1. In the Value (Y) Series box, click next to the series (1st, 2nd, 3rd, and so on) you want to label.

  2. Type a range reference or range name for the cells containing the labels.

  3. Repeat these steps for each value series you want to label.

■ To label a single value series at a time,

1. Highlight the spreadsheet cells containing the labels and copy the contents to the Clipboard with the Spreadsheet's Copy command.

2. Switch to the chart and choose the Data Labels command.

3. Click in the box next to the series you want to label and click the Paste button in the lower right corner of the dialog box.

Adding data labels to pie charts

When you work with a pie chart, choosing the Data Labels command produces the dialog box below. You can add any of several types of data labels to each slice of the pie:

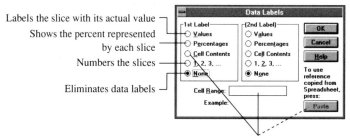

Labels the slice with its actual value
Shows the percent represented by each slice
Numbers the slices
Eliminates data labels

Labels the slices with the contents of the cells shown in the Cell Range box. If you've copied cell contents to the Clipboard, you can paste the range into the Cell Range box by clicking Paste.

Click an option in the 1st Label box to add a single label, such as the name of the category; click in the 2nd Label box to add a second data label, such as the percent the slice represents.

Fonts, Font Sizes, and Font Styles

You can specify two separate fonts, font sizes, and font styles in a chart. One set of options affects the main title only; the second affects all other text—subtitle, data labels, legends, and text on the vertical axes.

To format a title,

1. Choose Title Font from the Format menu. This dialog box appears:

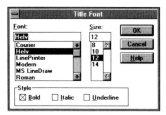

2. Click in the appropriate boxes to choose the font, size, and style or combination of styles you want.

To format other text, choose the Other Font command from the Format menu. This command produces a dialog box with the same options as the Title Font dialog box. Click in the Font, Size, and Style boxes to format the other text in your chart.

Patterns and Colors

When you create a chart, Works uses a standard set of colors, patterns (for black and white displays), and markers (for line charts). The program's choices are excellent, but on occasion you might prefer to put together and use a different set. To do this, choose the Patterns & Colors command on the Format menu.

If you're working with a bar or line chart, the following dialog box appears. (Pie charts are described later.)

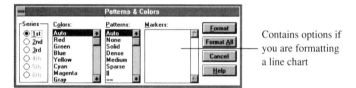

Contains options if you are formatting a line chart

For each series you want to change,

- Click in the Series box to indicate the value series for which you want to change the color, pattern, or marker.

- Click in the Colors box to choose a color for the series. *Auto* refers to the colors Works uses by default.

- Click in the Patterns box to choose a pattern. Again, *Auto* refers to the default patterns. Dense, Medium, and Sparse patterns produce screened effects made by patterns of dots. Scroll down through the Patterns box to see ×s, diagonal lines, and other choices.

- If you want to change the markers in a line chart, choose from the options in the Markers box.

To apply your changes,

- Click Format to affect a single series.

- Click Format All to affect all series.

- Click Close (labeled Cancel until you click either Format or Format All) to finish up.

If you're working with a pie chart, a somewhat different dialog box appears:

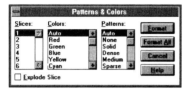

For each slice you want to affect,

■ Choose the slice in the Slices box.

■ Choose a color or pattern in the Colors and Patterns boxes.

■ Click the Explode Slice box to explode the slice away from the rest of the pie.

Click the Format, Format All, and Close buttons as described above to apply your changes.

Adjusting Axes

In addition to specifying fonts, styles, and colors or patterns, you can refine a bar, line, or scatter chart by adjusting its X-axis and Y-axis, by adding a second vertical axis on the right side, and by adding gridlines that help your viewer read the chart.

Adjusting the horizontal axis

To adjust the horizontal axis, choose the Horizontal (X) Axis command on the Format menu. If you're working with a bar or line chart, this dialog box appears:

■ Click in the Show Gridlines box to add vertical gridlines to your chart.

■ Click in the Label frequency box and type a number to change the labeling on the X-axis. The proposed value, 1, labels each category. Typing 2 labels every other category. You can use this option to keep labels on the X-axis from overlapping. Changing the frequency to 2, 3, 5, or some other interval is also a useful means of eliminating clutter when labels form an easily recognized series, such as year numbers.

NOTE: *If you're working on a scatter chart, the Horizontal Axis dialog box offers additional options. Use them to set the minimum and maximum values on the scale, to alter the interval between values, and to choose a logarithmic scale (powers of 10).*

Adjusting the vertical axis

When Works creates a chart with a vertical axis, it scales the axis according to the smallest and largest values you've chosen to plot. To adjust the vertical axis, choose Vertical (Y) Axis from the Format menu. This dialog box appears:

Changes the scale of the axis. Auto lets Works set the scale.

Adds horizontal gridlines

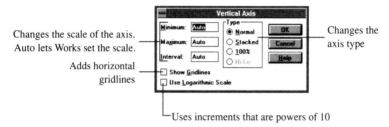

Changes the axis type

Uses increments that are powers of 10

The options in the Type box adjust the axis for variations of the chart type: Stacked shows the values stacked on one another to produce a cumulative total; 100% shows the values in relation to a 100% scale; Hi-Lo shows the relationship between minimum and maximum values.

Adding a second axis

On some charts you might find a second axis useful. You can add a second axis that shows either the same scale or a different one. To add a second (right) vertical axis:

1. Choose the Two Vertical Axes command from the Format menu. This dialog box appears:

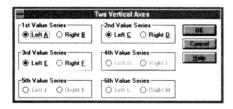

2. Click the Right button for whichever value series you want to scale against a right vertical axis. To create a right axis identical to the left one, click the right button in all active value-series boxes.

Once you've created a second vertical axis, you can adjust it with the Right Vertical Axis command (on the Format menu), which produces a

dialog box identical in content to the one you see when you choose the
Vertical (Y) Axis command.

MANAGING CHARTS

Works can associate up to eight charts with a single spreadsheet. These
charts are independent in the sense that you can view, change, and print
them; but in other respects they remain "attached" to the spreadsheets
from which they're generated. You cannot, for example, save a chart as
a file in its own right, nor can you open it without opening the spreadsheet first.

Although you don't have quite the "hands-on" capability with charts
that you do with letters, spreadsheets, and other documents, Works provides three commands on the Charts menu with which you can keep
track of your charts and clear away those you don't need:

■ Name lets you name a chart, replacing the default *Chart*X with something a little more descriptive. You can type up to 15 characters, including spaces:

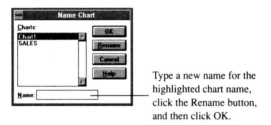

Type a new name for the
highlighted chart name,
click the Rename button,
and then click OK.

■ Delete lets you delete a chart—you can get rid of a chart you don't
want or remove an existing chart to make room for a new one.

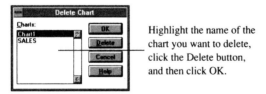

Highlight the name of the
chart you want to delete,
click the Delete button,
and then click OK.

■ Duplicate lets you make a copy of an existing chart. It produces a
dialog box that is almost identical to the Name Chart dialog box, described above. Highlight the chart you want to duplicate, and then
type a new name for the chart in the Name box. Click the Duplicate
button to make the copy, and click OK to carry out the command.

NOTE: *In the dialog boxes for the Name, Delete, and Duplicate commands, be sure to click the action button before you click OK. If you click OK without first clicking the action button, no change occurs.*

PRINTING A CHART

Printing a chart is based on the same skills you use in other Works applications. The following brief descriptions cover charting-specific options. For more information on printing, refer to Chapter 4.

Page Setup

To define your overall page layout before printing, choose the Page Setup & Margins command on the File menu. In the resulting dialog box, specify the margins, page size, and beginning page number in the appropriate boxes. Use the options in the Size box, described below, to control the size of your printed chart:

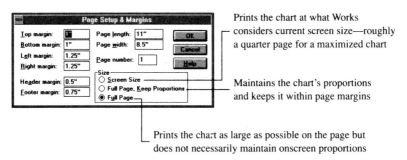

Prints the chart at what Works considers current screen size—roughly a quarter page for a maximized chart

Maintains the chart's proportions and keeps it within page margins

Prints the chart as large as possible on the page but does not necessarily maintain onscreen proportions

Seeing What You'll Get

If you have a color screen but a noncolor printer, the colors in your charts will be transformed into black-and-white patterns on paper. To see what the printed patterns will look like (for the current chart), choose Display As Printed from the Options menu. When a check mark appears to the left of this option, Works displays your chart with the default patterns, as it will be printed. To modify the patterns, use the Patterns & Colors command on the Format menu.

To check the printed size and layout of your chart, headings, and margins, click the Print Preview button on the Toolbar or choose Print Preview from the File menu.

When you're satisfied, click the Print button on the Toolbar or in the preview window, or choose the Print command from the File menu.

CHAPTER 8

Database Basics

A database, like a phone book, a catalog, or a cookbook, is any collection of records that gives you the basic facts: who, what, where, when, or, as is often the case, how much. Whenever you need to keep track of facts, the Works Database can help you organize, list, and sort them. With the Database, you can enter and sift through as many as 32,000 records per file. You can flip through the records one by one, like cards in a card file, or you can display or print them in rows, one after the other like troops on parade. This chapter tells you how to

- Create a database
- Work with different database *views*
- Sort a database alphabetically or numerically
- Query a database to find records that match certain criteria
- Preview and print a database

Chapter 9 tells you how to produce customized reports from a database.

STARTING THE DATABASE

To start the Database application, you can do either of the following:

- Click the Database button in either the Startup or the Create New File dialog box.
- Choose an existing database file (with the extension WDB) either from the list of recently used files at the bottom of the File menu or from the list displayed in the Open Existing File dialog box.

THE DATABASE SCREEN

If you choose to create a new file in the Database, the file is initially displayed in *form view*, as shown in Figure 8-1. You use form view to lay out an onscreen version of a paper-based form, complete with blanks in which you later enter your data.

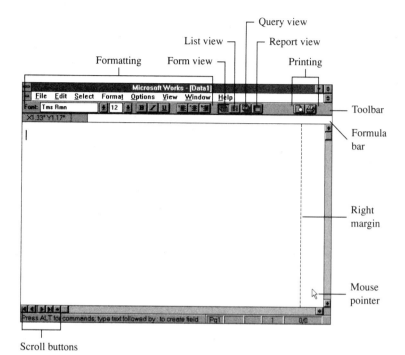

FIGURE 8-1. *The opening screen with the application and document windows maximized.*

At the top of the screen is the Toolbar. The formatting buttons on the Toolbar let you quickly specify the font (typeface) and font size, as well as any font styles (boldfacing, italics, underlining) and alignment you want. The printing buttons give you fast access to the Works preview and print features. The remaining buttons are your means of skipping from one database view to another:

■ Form view, as mentioned, is where you create a Works version of a paper form, like this:

■ List view is where you display multiple records on a grid formed, like a spreadsheet, of intersecting rows and columns of cells:

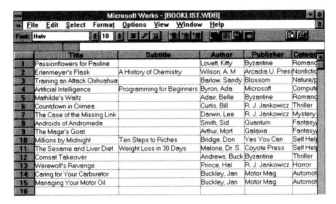

■ Query view is form view with an important difference: It's where you fashion *queries* that tell Works how you want to sort a database so that you can view or print only selected records.

■ Report view, covered in Chapter 9, is where you construct and customize a report for printing.

CREATING A DATABASE

A good way to become comfortable with the Database is to view yourself as an architect. You start by designing a structure (your form), and then you fill in the details (enter your data). As your "building" begins to take shape, you look at it from different angles (views), modifying and enhancing what you see until form and function combine to show you the data you need in the way you want to have it available.

Just as an architect must know about blueprints and drafting, you start by learning about *records* and *fields*:

■ A record is a collection of information that makes up a single database entry. For example, all the information about the book *Caring for Your Carburetor* makes up a single record in the sample database BOOKLIST.WDB, shown earlier. The same kinds of information about *Werewolf's Revenge* constitute another record.

■ A field represents one item in a record. In the book list example, for instance, the title makes up one field and the author's name another.

When you create a database, you begin by laying out a form that contains all the fields you need in order to hold the information you want to store about any record in your database. Although it's simple enough to create a form, you should avoid hitting the keyboard immediately. Take the time to think about what kinds of information you want to keep:

■ What are the most important fields in your database? You'll probably want to group some fields together and place the most important ones at or near the top.

■ What is the maximum number of fields you need for any single record? Even if only one record requires that you note, say, an author's Pulitzer Prize, you must create a field for the note when you design the form.

■ How, eventually, will you want to sort your database? You sort a database alphabetically or numerically by field, so break your entries into the smallest categories you think will be useful without fragmenting the data unnecessarily.

Creating a Form

After you decide the layout of your form, you can create the form in either form view or list view. Of the two, however, you'll probably find form view easier to work with. As in the Spreadsheet, Works displays your current entry in the formula bar beneath the Toolbar:

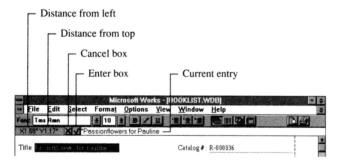

The Cancel box and Enter box are mouse-oriented equivalents of the Esc and Enter keys. The X and Y measurements displayed at the left edge of the formula bar help you position fields precisely, both in relation to each other and to the left and top edges of the paper.

To create a database field,

1. Position the blinking vertical insertion point where you want the field to be. Avoid positioning fields to the right of the broken vertical line, which marks the right margin of your page. Fields to the right of this line might not be printable.

2. Type a field name, followed by a colon (:). The field name can be up to 15 characters long. Don't forget the colon.

3. Press Enter or click the Enter box on the formula bar. When you do either, this dialog box appears:

4. Type the width, in characters, that you want the field to be. If you want a multiple-line field (a Notes section, for example), type the number of lines in the Height box. Click OK to complete the command.

Follow the same four steps for each field you want to create. You can create fields above, below, or to the side of other fields, but bear this in mind: When you switch to list view, Works will arrange the fields from left to right in the same order you created them. Try to create the fields in a sequence you'll be happy with when you see your records laid out in list view.

Modifying a Form

While working in form view, you can move fields around to improve the layout. You can also change field sizes and add headings or explanatory text (for example, instructions on how to fill out a certain field).

Alignment Aids

When you work in form view, Works helps you align fields by "snapping" them to an invisible grid on the screen. This grid, along with the coordinates displayed in the formula bar, makes it easy to ensure that fields are aligned exactly, either horizontally or vertically. If you are working on a complex form, however, or if you simply prefer more precise control over your layout, you can turn off the grid by opening the Options menu and choosing Snap To Grid. When a checkmark no longer appears next to this option, you can position fields with an accuracy of 0.01 inch. If you need this level of precision, use the direction keys to move fields. Only a very steady hand can rely on the mouse.

Moving fields on a form

To modify a form by moving fields,

1. Click on the field to select it. If you're using the keyboard, tab to the field you want and choose the Position Field command from the Edit menu. Either way, a small hand appears:

2. With the mouse, drag the field to its new location. On the keyboard, use the direction keys to move the field. As you work, a dotted outline moves onscreen. Release the mouse button or press Enter when the outline is where you want the field to be.

Altering field sizes in a form

To change the size of a field, you can—as usual—use either the mouse or the keyboard. With the mouse,

1. Click on the field to select it.

2. Move the mouse pointer until it is on the small, light square in the lower right corner of the field. When the pointer is correctly positioned, it becomes a slanting, two-headed arrow:

3. Drag to the left or right until the field is the size you want and then release the mouse button.

To change field sizes with the keyboard,

1. Tab to the field you want to change.

2. Choose the Field Size command from the Format menu.

3. When the Field Size dialog box appears, type the new width, measured in character spaces. Press Enter or click OK to complete the command.

Adding text to a form

Many printed forms contain headings, instructions, and explanations. You can easily add the same types of text to your form. Basically, text is different from a field name only in that it *doesn't* end with a colon:

1. Position the insertion point.

2. Type the text, and forget to type a colon at the end.

Entering Data

You can enter data either in form view or, as described later, in list view. In form view, you concentrate on one record at a time:

1. Highlight the dotted line to the right of a field name either by clicking on the line with the mouse or moving the highlight with the Tab key (Shift-Tab to move backward toward the top of the form).

2. Type the data you want in that field. (You can also enter formulas for making calculations automatically; for details, see "Formulas and Functions" later in this chapter.)

3. Click with the mouse or use the Tab key to highlight the next field.

4. When you reach the last field of one form and want to move on to a new one, press the Tab key. The highlight will appear in the first field of a new, blank form. When you finish the last entry in your last form, press Enter or click the Enter box (the one with the check mark) in the formula bar.

Protecting a Form and Your Data

After you've spent a lot of time creating a form, chances are you'll want to ensure that it can't be accidentally modified. From form view, open the Options menu. If a check mark is displayed next to Protect Form, protection is turned on. If you don't see a check mark, click the option.

When a form is protected, Works prohibits changes to the form itself, but you can enter and edit data, as well as add and delete records all you want. If you need to turn protection off (to modify the form), open the Options menu and click Protect Form again.

Protecting data is a little more elaborate because it involves both locking and protecting your data. Locking is actually more like installing a deadbolt: It makes protection *possible* but does not actually do anything.

To keep your data safe, you must turn on protection just as you would physically lock the deadbolt.

Initially, Works locks all fields, so to protect an entire database, you just turn protection on by choosing Protect Data from the Options menu. Note, however, that this works *only* if you have not tampered with the default locking. If you're unsure, follow the steps outlined below.

To protect data in certain fields (or in a database where you've turned locking on and off),

1. Open the Options menu and verify that both Protect Data and Protect Form are turned *off.*
2. Highlight the field or fields you want to protect.
3. Choose the Style command on the Format menu. When the following dialog box appears, verify that Locked is turned on, and click OK.

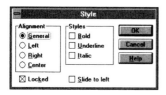

4. *Now* choose Protect Data from the Options menu.

To turn off data protection for a field, select the field and turn off Protect Data.

Viewing Records in Form View

Although you work with one record at a time in form view, Works gives you a special set of tools for flipping back and forth in the "stack." These tools appear alongside the horizontal scroll bar, in the lower left portion of the window:

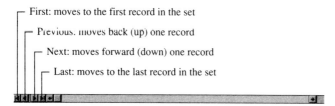

NOTE: *Although you might expect the Last button to take you to the last actual record, it in fact takes you to a blank new record following the last record that contains data.*

The right side of the status bar also helps you in form view by showing where the current record falls in relation to the first and last records you're displaying:

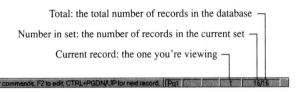

Total: the total number of records in the database ⌐

Number in set: the number of records in the current set ⌐

Current record: the one you're viewing ⌐

ALT for commands; F2 to edit; CTRL+PGDN/UP for next record. │Pg1│ │ │ 1 │ │ 16/16 │

The number of records in the set tells you how many records you're viewing out of the total number in the database. This number is the same as the total if you're viewing all records but if, as described later, you query the database to display only a selected subset, this number tells you how many out of the total match your criteria.

WORKING IN LIST VIEW

As you work with databases, especially large ones, you'll often find yourself switching to list view for the "big picture." When you want to work in list view, you can do either of the following:

■ Click the List button (second from the left) in the view section of the Toolbar.

■ Press F9 or choose List from the View menu.

Visually, the distinction between form view and list view is simple: As shown earlier, list view looks like a sheet of ledger paper and displays many records in a grid of cells. Each column in this grid represents a separate field, and each of the numbered rows holds a single record. If you're familiar with the Spreadsheet application, you'll notice that list view is like a spreadsheet in many ways. If you're not familiar with the Spreadsheet, you might find it helpful to scan Chapter 6. In particular, refer to the sections on the Fill commands, formatting, and formulas.

Adjusting Your Form in List View

If you switch to list view from form view, your first look might take you somewhat by surprise:

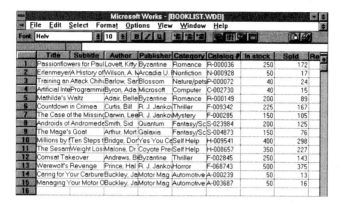

What happened to the column widths you so carefully set up in form view? Nothing. They're still there—in *form* view. In list view, Works defaults to 10-character column widths, just as it does in the Spreadsheet. When you switch to list view:

■ Field names, data, and formatting—such as italics or the display of numbers as currency or percents—transfer exactly.

■ Column widths, fonts, font sizes, headings, and explanatory text do not carry over.

Adjusting column widths

To change column widths in list view,

■ Place the mouse pointer on the boundary between two column heads, as shown below, and drag left to narrow the column, right to widen it.

Mouse pointer in position
to resize the Title column

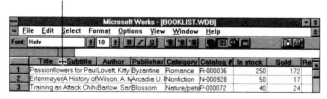

■ Or, choose the Field Width command from the Format menu. Type the column width, measured in characters, and click OK.

Adjusting fonts and font sizes

In list view, you can display and print additional rows and columns by changing to a different font or size. Simply click the downward-pointing arrow to the right of the Font or size boxes in the Toolbar.

Choose a new font name or font size from the list that opens.

Moving the Highlight in List View

If you have a mouse, moving the highlight and selecting cells in list view is simple:

■ Move the highlight by clicking the cell you want.

■ Select (highlight) two or more cell entries for copying, deletion, or formatting by dragging over the appropriate cells.

If you use the keyboard, the following table will help you maneuver quickly from field to field:

Key or Combination	Moves the Highlight
An arrow key	One cell in the indicated direction
Home	To the first field in the current row
End	To the last defined field in the current row
Ctrl-Home	To the first field in the first row
Ctrl-End	To the last defined field in the last row that contains data
Ctrl-Up	To the first row in the current field
Ctrl-Down	To the last row containing a record in the current field
PgUp, PgDn	Up or down one screen

When you want to select a block of field entries, use the key combinations in the following table:

Key Combination	Extends the Highlight
Shift-F8	An entire column
Ctrl-F8	An entire row
F8 and a direction key	One cell in that direction
Shift-Home	To the first field in the current row
Shift-End	To the last defined field containing data in the current row
Ctrl-Shift-Up or Down	Up or down to the first or last row containing records in the current field

Creating a Database in List View

Although list view is best for viewing and editing records, you can also use it to create a quick, simple database. To create fields in list view,

1. Highlight a cell in the column that is to become a field.

2. Choose the Field Name command from the Edit menu to produce a simple dialog box.

3. Type a field name of up to 15 characters. You do not have to type a colon at the end as you do in form view. Click OK to create the field.

Entering data in list view works much as it does in the Spreadsheet:

1. Click with the mouse or use the direction keys to highlight the cell in which you want to enter data.

2. Type the entry.

3. Use the mouse or direction keys to highlight a different cell if you want to continue entering data. Press Enter or click the Enter box in the formula bar to move on to another task.

FORMATTING

The Format menu, accessible from both form view and list view, lets you apply numeric formats, such as currency displays, and character styles, such as italics. You can also align entries to the left, center, or right in their fields.

When you apply formatting, it's important to remember that you format a field, not the entry in it. That means you can format a field once, and every entry in every record containing that field will have the formatting you specified.

Reentry Aids

Many databases contain fields in which the same information is repeated in one record after another. A database of local customers, for example, most likely contains recurring entries for city and, especially, state. One way you can simplify data entry is to use the Fill Down, Fill Right, and Fill Series commands. Another way is to use a formula to fill in the blanks for you. Formulas are described later, in the section "Formulas and Functions." The Fill commands, which appear in both the Spreadsheet and the Database, are described in Chapter 6 under the heading "Using the Fill Commands."

To apply formatting,

1. Highlight the field you want to format. If you're working in list view, you can highlight any cell in the field.

2. Choose the type of formatting you want, either from the Toolbar or from the Format menu, as described in the next few sections.

Number Formats

Most of the Format menu is devoted to number formats:

The number formats in the Database are the same as those you can use in the Spreadsheet. The following table lists the formats and shows what they look like. If you need more information, refer to the section "Formatting Numbers" in Chapter 6, page 93.

Format	Description	Examples
General	Integers and decimal fractions; exponential notation for entries too wide for field	123, 12.3, 1.23E+05
Fixed	Decimals rounded to fixed number of places	123.43 for 123.4321 rounded to two decimals
Currency	Currency values	$123.43
Percent	Percents	12.3% for .123, not 12.3
Exponential	Scientific notation	1.23E+03 for 1234
Leading Zeros	Zeros to the left to fill out specified number of digits	00123 for 123 padded to five digits
True/False	Displays TRUE in fields with nonzero values; FALSE in fields containing 0	TRUE for 123, FALSE for 0
Time/Date	Time or date	Numerous formats; see "Time/Date formats"

Choosing most number formats leads to a dialog box. Except for Leading Zeros and Time/Date, this is the dialog box you see:

Type the number of
decimal places you want.

If you choose the Leading Zeros format, the dialog box is almost identical to the one above: In the text box, type the number of digits you want displayed.

Time/Date formats

The Time/Date format produces a more elaborate, but still simple, dialog box:

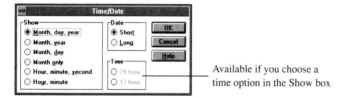

Available if you choose a
time option in the Show box

These are the possible combinations you can choose from the Show, Date, and Time boxes:

Format	Example
Month, day, year (short)	12/25/92
Month, day, year (long)	December 25, 1992
Month, year (short)	12/92
Month, year (long)	December 1992
Month, day (short)	12/25
Month, day (long)	December 25
Month only (short)	(Not available)
Month only (long)	December
Hour, minute, second (24 hour)	18:30:45
Hour, minute, second (12 hour)	6:30:45 PM
Hour, minute (24 hour)	18:30
Hour, minute (12 hour)	6:30 PM

Styles and alignments

Works lets you align field entries and apply font styles to them—boldface, italics, and underlining. Applying these formats is simple.

1. Highlight the field you want to format, in either list view or form view.

2. Click one of the following buttons on the Toolbar:

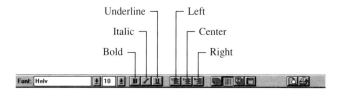

Or choose the Style command from the Format menu. Choose the formatting you want from the dialog box that appears.

FORMULAS AND FUNCTIONS

Suppose your database form includes fields that contain calculated values, like this:

Or perhaps the database contains data that appears in the same field in record after record:

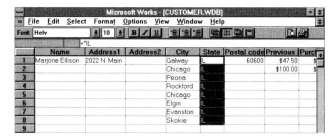

You can use formulas to make Works fill in the blanks:

- If a field contains the result of a calculation—the previous balance plus current purchases minus any received payment—one formula can produce the required calculation in every record in the database.

- If a field almost always contains the same entry, a simple non-mathematical formula can fill in the field for you, leaving you the much less repetitive task of typing only those entries that need changing.

Calculations

You can make Works do arithmetic by using either of the following:

- A formula you construct yourself
- A built-in function

NOTE: *The basics of using formulas and functions are described in Chapter 6 under the heading, "Creating Formulas" on page 97. This chapter doesn't duplicate that information, so refer to Chapter 6 if you need information about formulas, mathematical operators, and ways to control multiple calculations in a single formula.*

To create a formula for calculating,

1. Click on or tab to the field where you want the result displayed, in either list view or form view.

2. Begin the formula by typing an equal sign (=).

3. Create the formula, using field names to tell Works where to find the values to calculate:

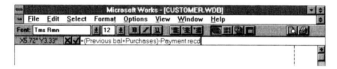

4. Press Enter or click the Enter box to complete the formula.

If you want to use a built-in function, refer to Appendix B for a list of functions and their correct formats.

Filling in the Blanks

Telling Works to fill a specific field in all records with the same text or value is really simple:

1. Click in or tab to the field where you want to enter the information, in either list view or form view.

2. Type an equal sign (=), followed by the entry. If the entry is a number, simply type the digits: *=98072*. If the entry is text, such as *Woodinville*, precede the text with a double quotation mark ("): *"Woodinville*.

If you use a formula to fill in a field, you can easily replace any occurrence that needs changing:

1. Highlight the entry.

2. Type the replacement.

3. Press Enter or click the Enter box.

EDITING, INSERTING, AND DELETING

A database is only as good as it is current, so periodic updates become a fact of life. Although Works can't control the quantity of data that needs changing, it can help you edit field entries as well as insert or delete records and fields.

Editing Field Entries

You replace or insert field entries simply by typing or retyping. To edit a field entry by inserting new characters or deleting old ones,

1. Highlight the field entry.

2. With the mouse, click in the formula bar at the position you want to edit:

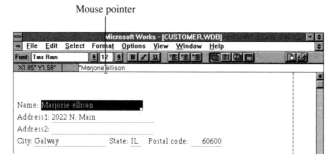

Mouse pointer

With the keyboard, press F2 to turn Works' attention to the formula bar, and use the arrow keys to position the insertion point.

3. To insert characters, type them. To delete characters, press Del. To replace characters, highlight them by dragging or by holding down

the Shift key and pressing an arrow key. Replace the highlighted characters by typing.

To delete a field entry,

1. Highlight the field entry.
2. Choose Clear Field Entry from the Edit menu. Alternatively, press Del and then press Enter or click the Enter box in the formula bar.

Inserting and Deleting Records

Both form view and list view offer Insert and Delete commands that affect whole records. To insert a new record,

- In form view, move to the record that is to follow the new record. Choose Insert Record from the Edit menu.
- In list view, click on the row number of the record that is to follow the new record. Choose Insert Record/Field from the Edit menu.

Either method causes Works to insert a blank, new record in front of the record or row you selected. All subsequent records or rows are automatically renumbered.

To delete a record,

- In form view, move to the record you want to delete. Choose Delete Record from the Edit menu.
- In list view, click on the row number of the record to delete. Choose Delete Record/Field from the Edit menu.

Fields

You can add and delete fields even after you've created a form and entered your data. If you want to add a new field, consider working in form view because it gives you more control over positioning. Create the field in the same way that you add fields to a new form.

If you want to work in list view, you add a new field to a blank column as follows:

1. Click on any cell in the column.
2. Choose Field Name from the Edit menu and type the name of the new field in the dialog box that appears. Click OK.

To insert a new field between other fields in list view,

1. Click the field name at the top of the column that's located to the right of the field-to-be.

2. Choose Insert Record/Field from the Edit menu to insert a new column (field).

3. Choose the Field Name command from the Edit menu and name the new field.

NOTE: *When you insert fields in list view and then switch to form view, the new field appears at the top of your form, possibly overlying an existing field. To untangle the fields, move the new field with the mouse or keyboard.*

When you delete a database field, you also delete the information it contains in all your records, so think carefully before removing existing fields. If you find that a field must be deleted, use form view:

1. Choose Delete Field from the Edit menu. If the field contains data, you see this warning:

2. If you're sure you want to lose the information, click OK.

NOTE: *You can also delete a field in list view, but you receive no warning message if the field contains data. The command is carried out immediately, so delete with care.*

WORKING WITH A DATABASE

A small database of 20 or so records is easy to display in list view. A larger database, however, could have you scrolling instead of working most of the time. Or at least it could if you didn't have a number of commands that help you view, search, and sort a database, as well as display selected records.

Jumping with Go To

You can use the Go To command either to move to a specific record or to move quickly from one field to another. Go To is available in both form view and list view:

1. Press F5 or choose Go To from the Select menu. This dialog box appears:

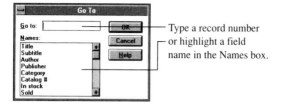

Type a record number
or highlight a field
name in the Names box.

2. If you want a specific record, type the record number in the Go To box. Click OK or press Enter. In form view, the record immediately appears on the screen. In list view, the highlight jumps up or down in the current field, landing on the record you seek.

If you want to move to a particular field, highlight the field name in the Names box. Click OK or press Enter. The highlight immediately moves to the specified field in the current record.

Highlighting with Find

The Find command searches your database for a set of characters you specify, numbers or text. You can use the Find command for either of two purposes: to find the next occurrence of the characters you specify, or to find and display only the records that contain those characters.

You can use the Find command in either form view or list view. To use the command:

1. Choose Find from the Select menu. A dialog box appears asking what you want to find:

Type the text
you want to find.

2. Type the characters you seek, uppercase or lowercase. You can type less than a complete entry, but type enough to weed out similar entries: Typing *bus* causes Works to find not only *bus*, but *Business*, *busy, BUST,* and *bush.*

3. In the Match box, choose Next Record if you simply want Works to move the highlight to the next set of matching characters. Choose All Records if you want Works to sort through the records and display only those that contain the characters you specified, as shown below. To redisplay the full set of records, choose Show All Records on the Select menu.

	Subtitle	Author	Publisher	Category	Catalog #	In stock
6		Curtis, Bill	R. J. Jankowicz	Thriller	F-009342	229
12		Andrews, Buck	Byzantine	Thriller	F-002845	250
16						

Microsoft Works - [BOOKLIST.WDB]
File   Edit   Select   Format   Options   View   Window   Help
Font: Helv   10   B I U
"Thriller

Sorting Records

With the Sort Records command, you can arrange records either alphabetically or numerically according to the entries in up to three fields.
The easiest way to think of Sort Records is to visualize the type of
alphabetizing in your telephone directory, as reflected in the following
sample database:

Field 1   Field 2   Field 3

Microsoft Works - [NAMES.WDB]
File   Edit   Select   Format   Options   View   Window   Help
Font: Helv   10   B I U

	Last name	First name	Middle	Phone			
1	Jaworsky	Allen	Z.	555-1234			
2	Jellico	Shirley		555-7560			
3	Jones	Casey	A.	555-8493			
4	Jones	Casey	Lee	555-9054			
5	Jones	Casey	Ronald	555-7102			
6	Jones	Charlene		555-2847			
7	Jones	Charles		555-1945			
8							

More Matchmaking

If you're familiar with the MS-DOS wildcard characters ? and *, you'll
be glad to know you can use them with the Find command, too. As
usual, the question mark can stand for any other single character; the
asterisk can stand for any number of other characters. It's important to
remember, however, that the Works Find command does *not* distinguish
between whole words and parts of words. Thus, *b?d* finds not only *bad*,
bed, and *bud*, but also *budget* and *ombudsman*. Similarly, *b*d* finds any
combination from *bad* to *ballooned*, *rub down*, and *unbidden*. You can
limit a search to whole words by including a space before, after, or on
both sides of the search characters. Be sure, however, that such spaces
do, indeed, match spaces surrounding the characters you want to find.
If they do not, Works tells you *No match found*.

Each part of each person's name is represented as a database field. To sort the entries alphabetically, you would want to sort three fields:

- Field 1 to alphabetize last names (Jaworsky, Jellico, Jones).

- Field 2 to alphabetize the first names of people with the same last name (Casey, Charlene, and Charles Jones).

- Field 3 to alphabetize the middle names or initials of people with the same first and last names (Casey A. Jones, Casey Lee Jones, Casey Ronald Jones).

To sort a database,

1. In either list view or form view, choose the Sort Records command from the Select menu. (List view is preferable because you can see the results of the sort more easily.) In the subsequent dialog box, Works proposes the first field as the first sort field:

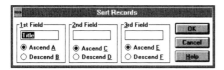

2. If the proposed response is not correct, type the name of the first field you want to sort.

3. If you want an ascending sort (A–Z or 0–9), leave the Ascend option turned on. For a descending sort (Z–A or 9–0), click Descend.

4. Enter field names and click Ascend or Descend for the second and third fields (if any) you want to sort. Click OK to sort the database.

Applying Queries

In addition to sorting a database, you can fashion queries that search out and display records that match very specific criteria. For example, you can search a database to find only those records with balances due greater than $500 *and* with payments 30 or more days late. Queries are at the heart of a database program, and this area is where you can really put Works through its paces. Unfortunately, queries—like formulas—depend so much on your own data that this book can give you only the basic procedures.

Query view

When you want to query a database, you enter query view in either of the ways mentioned on the next page.

■ Click the Query button on the Toolbar:

■ Choose Query from the View menu.

In appearance, query view looks like form view with a blank form on display. This view is, however, the one in which you type the criteria that tell Works which records you seek.

Simple queries

You can begin to fashion simple queries with very little database experience. All you do is follow these steps:

1. Enter query view.

2. Highlight a field and type the entry you seek. You can refine the query by typing entries in more than one field. For example:

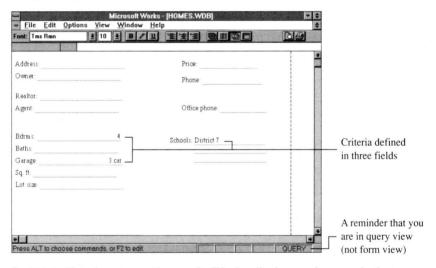

3. Switch to list view to see the result. Works displays only records that match in each field:

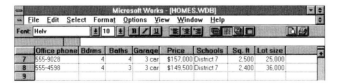

When you no longer want to limit the list to matching records, choose Show All Records from the Select menu.

NOTE: *If you use a date in a query, you must enclose it in single quotation marks, like this: '12/25/92'.*

Finding related records

When you want to broaden a query beyond exact matches, you can add mathematical operators to the entry you search for. The following table summarizes these operators; for more details, see Chapter 6 under the heading "Operators."

In the table that follows, the italicized words *number* and *text* stand for numbers and text you would supply. Notice that text *must* be enclosed in double quotation marks.

Operator	Use to Find
>*number*	All values greater than *number*. For example, >500 finds 501 and above.
<*number*	All values less than *number*. For example, <500 finds 499 and below.
>=*number*	All values greater than or equal to *number*. For example, >=500 finds 500 and above.
<=*number*	All values less than or equal to *number*. For example, <=500 finds 500 and below.
"*text*"	All entries that follow *text* in the alphabet. For example, >"C" finds all words and letters (including *cat* and *canary*) that follow the letter *C*.
<"*text*"	All entries that precede *text* in the alphabet. For example, <"C" finds all words and letters that precede the letter *C*.
>="*text*"	All entries greater than or equal to *text*. For example, >="C" finds the letter *C* and all letters and words that follow it in the alphabet.
<="*text*"	All entries less than or equal to *text*. For example, <="C" finds the letter *C* and all letters and words that precede it in the alphabet.
<>*number*	All entries that are not equal to *number*. For example, <>0 finds all nonzero entries.
<>"*text*"	All entries that are not equal to *text*. For example, <>"CA" finds all state abbreviations except California's.

Larger queries

Queries can sometimes look and act like formulas. The preceding section described the use of mathematical operators in queries. You can also incorporate calculations and built-in functions. You can, for example, design a query like this to find the records of all employees whose combined salary and bonus exceeded $50,000:

To design such a query,

1. Highlight the field you want to search.
2. Type an equal sign. If you don't, Works treats the formula as text.
3. Type the query, using field names and any of these operators:
   + (addition), − (subtraction), ∗ (multiplication), / (division),
   ^ (exponentiation).

NOTE: *Use parentheses as described in Chapter 6 in the section called "Controlling the Order of Evaluation" to control the way in which Works evaluates conditions or operations.*

Designing queries with AND and OR

Yet another query format lets you string a set of conditions together with the help of two additional operators, & (AND) or | (OR), as shown in the sample query below:

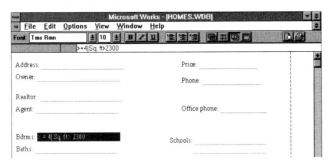

This format lets you

■ Specify a range. For example, typing *>=100000&<135000* in the Price field tells Works that you want to see all the records for houses costing $100,000 or more but less than $135,000.

■ Include alternatives in a search. For example, typing the condition *>=4| Sq. ft > 2300* lets you tell Works that you want all records in which the number of bedrooms is greater than 4 *or* the number of square feet is greater than 2300.

The net result is that & and | help you fashion queries that evaluate database records to find either those that meet two or more conditions or those that meet any of two or more conditions.

Showing and Hiding Records

When you apply queries to a database, Works displays only those records that match the criteria you specified. The rest are temporarily hidden. They don't have to stay that way, though. You can switch from the displayed records to the hidden records with a single command, in effect using a query to break your database into two "piles" of records.

After you define and apply a query,

■ Choose Switch Hidden Records from the Select menu (in either form view or list view) to see the records that *don't* match the criteria. To see the other set of records again, choose Switch Hidden Records a second time.

■ Choose Show All Records from the Select menu to view all records, effectively undoing your query. To reapply the query, press F3 or choose Apply Query from the Select menu.

You can also hide records temporarily—perhaps to keep them from casual view or to suppress them in a report.

■ To hide one or more records, highlight the records and choose Hide Record from the Select menu.

■ To redisplay the hidden records, choose Show All Records from the Select menu.

PRINTING A DATABASE

Although the Database report view helps you organize and print the records in your database, printing from form view or list view can be useful too, because each view gives you a printout that corresponds to the onscreen layout of your database. Printing from form view gives you forms; printing from list view gives you lists.

In either view, Works prints whatever database records are available for display, so

■ Choose Show All Records from the Select menu if you've applied a query that displays only some records but you want all of them available for printing.

■ Design and apply a query or hide specific records if you want to print only selected records.

Printing from Form View

When you print from form view, you can tailor the printout in any of several ways. To see and choose your options, choose the Page Setup & Margins command from the File menu. This dialog box appears:

Margins, headers, and page size are covered in Chapter 4. If you need help with these, refer to the sections beginning with ''Defining Page Layouts'' in that chapter. The options in this dialog box that are specific to form view are as follows:

■ Print Which Records lets you specify whether to print all displayable records or only the one currently displayed. To print a blank version of your form, display a blank form and click Current Record Only.

■ Page Breaks Between Records, which is turned on by default, prints each record on a separate page. To print more than one record on a page, turn this option off. You can then use the Space Between Records text box to tell Works how to space the records. The proposed response of 0", even though it sounds compact, is adequate for most purposes.

■ Print Field Lines tells Works to print the dotted lines that show the width of each field. Turn it on if you want the lines printed.

■ Print Which Items tells Works whether you want to print both field names and field entries (All Items) or field entries but no field names (Field Entries Only).

Printing from List View

Printing from list view is straightforward. To see your options, choose Page Setup & Margins. This dialog box appears:

The options specific to list view are as follows:

- Print Gridlines, which tells Works to print the horizontal and vertical gridlines you see onscreen.

- Print Record And Field Labels, which tells Works to print the field names at the top and the record (row) numbers down the left side.

Printing

Whichever view you choose to print from, use Print Preview (described in Chapter 4) to see what your printout will look like before you commit it to paper. To enter Print Preview, either

- Click the Preview button (second from the right) on the Toolbar.

- Or choose Print Preview from the File menu.

As in the other Works applications, you can use the Zoom buttons to enlarge your preview; the Next and Previous buttons let you move from one record to another. When you're ready to print, click the Print button in the Toolbar or in the preview window, or choose Print from the File menu. A simple dialog box appears:

Type the number of
copies you want to print.

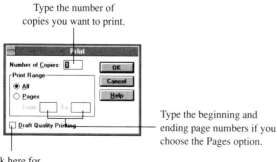

Type the beginning and
ending page numbers if you
choose the Pages option.

Click here for
a fast printout.

CHAPTER 9

Reporting Basics

The report generator works hand in hand with the Database to help you define and print reports that, in turn, help you analyze your data. How, you might wonder, does this differ from printing in the Database application itself? Generating reports, as you'll find in this chapter, gives you the flexibility you don't have when printing directly from the Database because you can

- Choose the fields you want to include
- Arrange those fields in any way you want
- Add titles, headings, and statistics
- Sort and summarize related records within the report
- Generate up to eight reports, each organized to suit a particular need for information

STARTING THE REPORT GENERATOR

After you create a database, you can start the report generator from form view, list view, or query view. If you've applied a query to display only certain records, the report you create will, at least initially, contain only those records. You can change the contents of the report at any time, however, by using another query or by using the Select menu in form view or list view to display all the records or a different subset.

To begin creating a report, open the database—here, the book list you looked at in Chapter 8. After you do so,

- Click the Report view button on the Toolbar:

┌─ Report view

- Or choose Create New Report from the View menu

DEFINING A REPORT

Your first look at the report generator is a large dialog box:

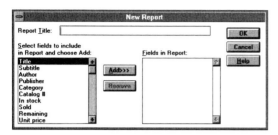

This is the first of two dialog boxes in which you *define* your report by telling Works how you want it constructed. Here, you build the framework of the report; in particular, you tell Works which fields you want to include, and the order in which you want them to appear. The following list describes the elements in the New Report dialog box:

- In the box labeled Report Title, you can type a title for the report. As described under the heading "Titles" later in this chapter, creating a title here is a convenience rather than a necessity because you can also title a report after you've created it.

- The list box headed Select Fields To Include contains the names of all the fields in your database. Choose the fields you want to include in your report.

  1. Highlight the field name in the list box.

  2. Click the button labeled Add.

     You can add as many or as few fields as you want. As you pick and choose, however, bear in mind that Works arranges fields in the report from left to right, beginning with the first field you added. Try to select the fields in the sequence you want to see.

- The Fields In Report box displays a list of the fields you've added to your report. If you want to remove a field name from this box,

  1. Highlight it.

  2. Click the Remove button.

When you've chosen all the fields you want, click OK. At this point, instead of seeing a report appear, you see a second dialog box, shown on the following page.

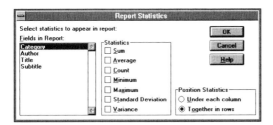

This box represents one of the most engaging features of the report generator. It's a built-in "prompt" that asks whether—and how—you want calculations (statistics) applied to your data. You can choose from a number of common calculations, including sums, averages, and counts (number of entries). Minimum and Maximum give you, respectively, the lowest and highest values in the field.

To choose statistics,

1. In the Fields In Report box, highlight the name of the field for which you want the statistic. This box lists the fields you chose to include in your report, rather than all the fields in your database.

2. Click the box next to the statistic you want. You can apply more than one statistic to a given field.

3. Repeat the preceding steps for each field you want to summarize.

4. Use the Position Statistics box to tell Works where to put the results of its calculations. Under Each Column displays and prints each statistic below the field to which it applies; Together In Rows collects all statistics in rows at the end of the report.

5. Click OK.

Now the report generator takes over and puts together the report you requested. When it finishes, you see yet another dialog box, which tells you that the *report definition* has been created.

Reports versus Report Definitions

When Works displays the results of generating a report, you don't immediately see rows and columns of data marching down the screen. You see a report definition that shows how your report is constructed.

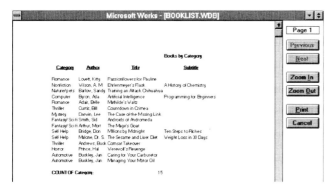

Because a report definition is so lean and clean, you can see past the "busy-ness" of your data to determine where and how you might want to modify or enhance the report. At the same time, you don't ever have to guess at how the definition will eventually organize and print your data, because Print Preview can display the results whenever you want. Here, for example, is the preceding report definition, before any cosmetic touchups, in Print Preview:

NOTE: *The Toolbar and most of the menu commands in report view are identical to the same features in the Database list view or form view. This chapter covers reporting only; for details on such features as Toolbar buttons, number formats, and queries, refer to Chapter 8.*

Parts of a Report Definition

A report definition looks a lot like a spreadsheet or a database in list view. As you can see in Figure 9-1, columns are familiarly labeled A, B, C, and so on. Rows, however, are named individually according to the information they contain:

■ Title—a title row, as you'd expect, holds a report title. Works prints a title only on the first page of a report.

- Headings—a headings row contains field names or other text you choose to head the columns in your report. Headings appear on every page of a report.

- Record—a record row contains field names, which are replaced by the field entries that normally make up the body of your report.

- Summary—a summary row contains statistics. Summaries appear at the end of the report.

- Intr *fieldname*—an Intr *fieldname* row is like a headings row, but it appears between groups of records in a sorted database. In a report definition, Works replaces *fieldname* with the name of an actual field.

- Summ *fieldname*—a Summ *fieldname* row is like a summary row, but it appears between sorted groups of records. Again, Works replaces *fieldname* with the name of a real field.

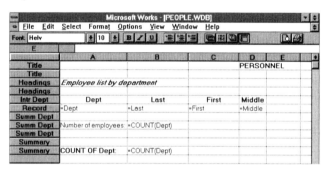

FIGURE 9-1. *This report definition shows all the row types.*

The following Print Preview window illustrates the way the row types appear in the report:

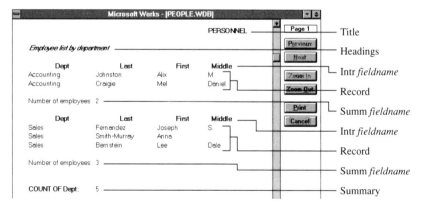

MODIFYING A REPORT

The report definition Works produces might be all you need for many reports. At times, however, you'll want to fine-tune the definition by inserting or deleting rows or columns, adding text, and—especially— grouping related records within the report.

Inserting a New Row

Although Works names the rows in your report, you can add a new one with ease simply by telling Works which type of row you want to insert:

1. Highlight the row *below which* you want to insert the new row. (To avoid an extra step, highlight the entire row by clicking on its name—Title, Headings, Record, and so on.)

2. Choose Insert Row/Column from the Edit menu. This dialog box appears:

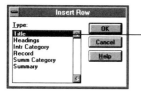 Works highlights the type of row you selected on the report. Click OK to insert a row of that type, or highlight a different type and click OK.

Works always groups rows of the same type and displays them in this sequence: Title, Headings, Intr *fieldname*, Record, Summ *fieldname*, and Summary. Thus, if you highlight one type of row and choose to insert a row of a different type, Works inserts the new row in the group to which it belongs. You cannot mix row types, nor should you ever feel the need to do so.

Inserting a New Column

Inserting a new, blank column is simple:

1. Highlight the column that you want to appear to the *right* of the new column. Save time by clicking on the alphabetic label (A, B, C) at the top of the column.

2. Choose Insert Row/Column from the Edit menu.

Deleting Rows and Columns

To delete one or more rows or columns, do the following:

1. Highlight the row(s) or column(s) to be deleted.

2. Choose Delete Row/Column from the Edit menu.

NOTE: *Bear in mind that if you delete a row or column containing part of the report definition, that information will no longer exist in the printed report.*

Adding and Replacing Text

When you create a report definition, Works normally

■ Boldfaces any title you type and attempts to center it on the page

■ Uses field names as column headings

■ Describes statistics with a line such as COUNT OF *fieldname*

After you've created the report definition, you can add text, explanations, and calculation formulas wherever you want:

1. If necessary, add a new row of the type you need.

2. If you're replacing text, highlight the unwanted entry. If you're adding text, highlight the cell where the text is to appear.

3. Type the entry and press Enter or click the Enter box (the one with the check mark) in the formula bar.

Titles

When you type a title in the New Report dialog box, Works can successfully center it on the printed page if your columns are close to the default column width of 10 characters. If your columns are either very narrow or very wide, however, the title can be thrown off center. In situations like this, you can try to center the title yourself in one of three ways:

■ By changing the font or font size if the title is just slightly off center.

■ By physically moving the title to the center column with the Cut and Paste commands or, simply, by deleting and retyping. If necessary, you can also try different alignments (left, center, right) to position the title more neatly.

■ By creating a centered header (as described in Chapter 4). In this case, however, your "title" will appear in the top margin of each page, rather than on the first page only.

If a centered title is not especially important, or if you want to add a title or subtitle after creating the report definition,

1. Add a Title row, if necessary.

2. Place the highlight in the column of your choice in the Title row, type the title, and press Enter or click the Enter box.

After you create a title, you can format and align it with the Toolbar or with the Font and Style commands on the Format menu. In reporting, as in your Database and Spreadsheet files, bear in mind that the font and font size you choose affect the entire report. You can apply font styles, such as boldface or italic, selectively—to parts of a report—but not fonts or sizes.

Selecting and Sorting Records

You can select and sort records in form view, list view, query view, or report view. The view you use and the approach you take depends on what you want your report to show.

■ If you want a report that includes selected records only, you can apply a query to your database. The result looks something like this:

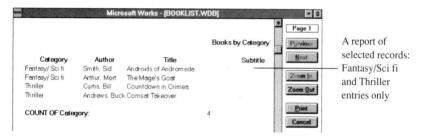

A report of selected records: Fantasy/Sci fi and Thriller entries only

■ If you want a report that arranges records in some type of order, you can sort the database in form view or list view to produce a report more like this:

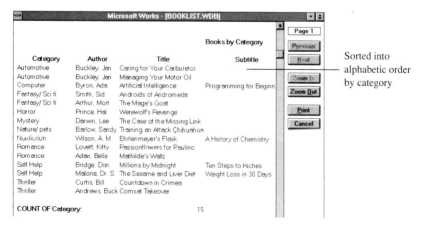

Sorted into alphabetic order by category

■ If you want a report that groups and summarizes records, you sort the database in report view, as shown on the next page.

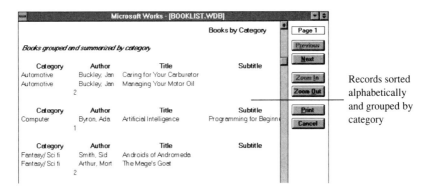

Records sorted
alphabetically
and grouped by
category

Chapter 8 describes how to sort and query databases, as illustrated in the first two examples. The following explanation refers to sorting in report view only:

1. Choose the Sort Records command from the Select menu. This dialog box appears:

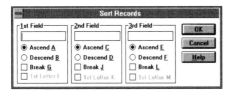

As in form view and list view, you can sort records on up to three fields, in ascending order (A to Z, or 0 to 9) or descending order (Z to A, or 9 to 0).

2. In the 1st, 2nd, and 3rd Field boxes, specify the field or fields you want to sort. For each, choose an ascending or descending sort.

3. To group the records, use the Break and 1st Letter options. Check Break for the appropriate field if you want to insert a break whenever any part of the field changes (for example, to break between Nature and Nonfiction). When you check Break, the 1st Letter option also becomes available. Check it if you want a less rigorous grouping that breaks only when the first letter in the field changes (to break between Mystery and Nature, for example, but not between Nature and Nonfiction).

4. Click OK to carry out the sort, and then click Print Preview to see the result.

When you choose the Break and 1st Letter options, Works inserts a Summ *fieldname* row between groups. It also creates statistics for each column: a count of text entries, or a sum of numeric data. To eliminate any statistics you don't want,

1. Highlight the statistic in the Summ *fieldname* row, like this:

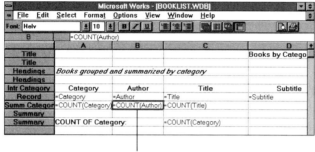

The highlighted field entry is a statistic that
counts (different) entries in the Author column.

2. Choose Clear from the Edit menu, or press Del followed by Enter.

Working with Fields

The Edit menu in report view includes three commands that can help you insert field names, field entries, and field statistics into a report definition. Using these commands, you can minimize typing as you create new columns and add statistics to a report or create formulas for calculating values.

Inserting field names and field entries

When you're working with a report definition, you use field *names* and field *entries* for totally different purposes. A field name is text; a field entry is an instruction to display or print the data entries in the field you specify.

You insert a field name when you want the name itself to appear in the report—for example, when you

- Add a new column to the report

- Include a field name in a formula, such as =Quantity*Price

- Use field names as headings *between* groups in a sorted report

NOTE: *If you insert field names as headings between groups (the third item above), avoid duplicate headings at the top of the page by deleting the Headings row. Add an Intr* fieldname *row to the report, and insert the field names in the Intr row.*

You insert a field entry when you want entries represented by the field to appear in the report. Because field entries represent data, you generally insert them in Record rows. For example, if you added a new column to a report, you would highlight the Record row in that column and insert the field entry to tell Works to include the data in your report.

Although their uses are dissimilar, you insert field names and field entries in much the same way·

1. Highlight the cell where you want the name or entry to appear and choose Insert Field Name or Insert Field Entry from the Edit menu. A dialog box like this appears:

2. Highlight the field name (or entry) you want and click OK.

Inserting field summaries

Field summaries let you add any of the standard report statistics for a field. The entries affected by the statistic depend on the type of row into which you insert the summary:

- If you insert a field summary in a Summ *fieldname* row (in a sorted report only), Works applies the statistic to each sorted group.

- If you insert a field summary in a Summary row, Works applies the statistic to all entries in the field.

To insert a field summary,

1. Insert a Summ *fieldname* row if necessary.

2. Highlight the cell where you want the summary to appear and choose Insert Field Summary from the Edit menu. This dialog box appears:

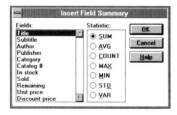

3. Choose the field you want to summarize from the Fields box and choose the statistic you want calculated from the Statistic box. Click OK to add the statistic to your report.

MANAGING REPORTS

Because you can create up to eight reports for a single database, you'll find that reports, like files and children, need supervision to avoid becoming unruly or going astray. Three commands on the report window's View menu help you stay in control: Name Report, Delete Report, and Duplicate Report. The three commands produce similar dialog boxes but differ greatly in purpose.

Assigning Names

When you create a report, Works gives it a generic name: Report1, Report2, Report3, and so on. To assign a more descriptive name,

1. Choose the Name Report command from the View menu. The following dialog box appears:

2. Highlight the report you want to name in the Reports box.

3. Click or press Tab to move to the Name box and type a name of up to 15 characters.

4. Click the Rename button, *not* OK. Works displays the new name in the Reports box; now click OK to close the dialog box.

Making Copies

To make an exact copy of a report—perhaps because you want to modify one version while keeping the original intact—use the Duplicate Report command:

1. Choose Duplicate Report from the View menu. A dialog box appears, as shown on the next page.

2. Highlight the report you want to duplicate in the Reports box. Now do either of the following:

   □ Click the Duplicate button to have Works create the copy and assign it a default (Report*x*) name.

   □ Move to the Name box, type a name for the copy, and then click Duplicate to create the copy and assign it the name you specified.

3. Click OK.

Eliminating Unneeded Reports

To delete an unneeded report or to cull one so that you can create a different report in its place,

1. Choose Delete Report from the View menu.

2. Highlight the report to delete in the Reports box:

3. Click the Delete button, *and then* click OK.

PRINTING A REPORT

After you've organized, sorted, grouped, and formatted your report, you can preview the results in Print Preview. When you're using Print Preview with a long report or a wide one spanning more than one page, notice where your pages break. If you want to break the report between other columns or between certain types of rows,

1. Return to report view. To break between columns, highlight a cell in the column to the right of the point at which you want a page break. To break between row types, highlight a cell in the row beneath the break point you want to establish.

2. Choose Insert Page Break from the Edit menu.

To set up page sizes, margins, and other elements of page layout, choose Page Setup & Margins from the Edit menu. The following dialog box appears:

Specify the margins, page size, and, if necessary, the first page number. Click Print All But Record Rows if you want to print headings, titles, and statistics but *no* records.

For the actual printing you can, as usual, click the Print button on the Toolbar (or in Print Preview) or choose Print from the File menu.

CHAPTER 10

Moving Data from Place to Place

There are three basic ways in which you might want to move data: between documents, between programs, and between computers. This chapter tells you about the first two. In particular, it covers

- Cutting, copying, and pasting within and between applications via the Clipboard
- Linking data to a word processed document
- Embedding charts, drawings, and other objects in a word processed document
- Working with the Database and the Word Processor to create mailing labels and form letters

The third way to move data, between computers, belongs in the realm of communications—very interesting, but not strictly a part of Works. If you have a modem and want to transfer data between computers, you can use the Windows accessory called Terminal with your Works files. Refer to your Windows manual and to Terminal's online Help for more information.

THREE WAYS TO MOVE DATA

The goal of data transfer is simple: to enable you to use your information whenever and wherever you want, without regard to document types or differences between applications. This goal is met by Works with the help of the Clipboard and two data-handling features called *linking* and *embedding*. All three move data, but they treat the data in different ways:

- The Clipboard acts as a temporary home for data you want to move or duplicate elsewhere. When you use the Cut, Copy, and Paste commands, the Clipboard acts as a receptacle for data in transit.

- Linking not only copies information from one application into another, it also establishes a link between the source and the copy. Works uses this link to update the copy automatically whenever you make changes to the source document. Linking within Works operates only from spreadsheets and charts to word processed documents.

- Embedding also transfers information from one application to another, but it inserts the data as a "lump" called an object. Embedded objects are not automatically updated, but a connection remains between them and their source applications. When you want to edit an embedded object, you use this connection to activate the source application.

NOTE: *The remainder of this chapter focuses on moving data between Works applications; however, Works can paste, link, and embed information from other Windows programs, such as Microsoft Excel, that support these capabilities.*

USING THE CLIPBOARD

The Clipboard, along with the Cut, Copy, and Paste commands, is the easiest means of moving data either between documents in the same application or between documents in different applications. As described in Chapter 4, you select the data and then do the following:

- Use Cut to move the data to the Clipboard, removing it from the source document.

- Use Copy (instead of Cut) to duplicate the data on the Clipboard, leaving it in the source document.

- Use Paste to insert the Clipboard contents at the insertion point in the document that is to receive the data.

Pasting in the Same Document or Application

When you want to paste information within the same application,

1. Select the information and cut or copy it to the Clipboard.

2. If you're pasting to a different document, open it.

3. Place the insertion point or highlight where you want the information inserted.

4. From the Edit menu, choose either the Paste command (Paste Record in the Database list view) or the Paste Special command. Paste inserts text, values, and formulas as you copied them to the Clipboard. Paste Special gives you additional options:

☐ In the Word Processor, the following dialog box enables you to paste character or paragraph *formatting* rather than the actual information on the Clipboard:

☐ In the Spreadsheet, a similar dialog box lets you paste values only (no formulas) or to add or subtract incoming values and existing values in the target cells:

Pasting Between Applications

Because Works is both a Windows program and integrated software, you can move data not only between documents but from one application to another simply by passing it along via the Clipboard.

Pasting to the Word Processor

Of the three main Works applications, the Word Processor is the most adept at accepting data. When you use the Paste command to move data to the Word Processor, Works makes a number of adjustments:

■ Spreadsheet contents emerge as rows and columns separated by tabs.

■ Database records in either form view or list view arrive in rows with fields separated by tabs.

■ Database reports (copied to the Clipboard with the report view Copy Report Output command) appear as they would be printed out, with fields separated by tabs.

Paste Special When you move data to the Word Processor from another application, the Paste Special dialog box is totally revamped:

Here, you have a choice of pasting the Clipboard contents in any of several data types:

■ Text and OemText, as you would expect, give you typical characters you can select, format, and edit individually. OemText, unlike Text, includes the full range of characters, including lines and accented letters, built into your computer.

■ Bitmap and Picture paste the Clipboard contents as graphic images you can select only as whole items. Both reproduce a "picture" of the chart or cells you copied to the Clipboard, complete with gridlines and (for charts) colors. Bitmap produces a more exact image than Picture, but it can slow down screen updates when you scroll.

■ Works Internal Format pastes the Clipboard contents as Works data.

■ MS Works Spreadsheet (which doesn't appear in the Data Type list box above) pastes and *links* incoming data to its source. For more about this data type, refer to "Linking Data" later in this chapter.

NOTE: *If you're pasting from a non-Works application, you might see some other data type, such as Rich Text Format. Programs rely on different "languages" to describe their data to one another. If you use such a data type and don't like the results, use Undo to eliminate the paste job and try a different data type.*

Pasting to the Spreadsheet and Database

When you paste data from the Word Processor to the Spreadsheet and Database, Works adjusts the formatting as follows:

■ A table with entries separated by tabs is pasted into equivalent rows and columns, one entry per cell or field.

■ A block of text is pasted into a single cell in the Spreadsheet and in Database list view, and into a single field in form view.

Pasting between the Spreadsheet and the Database

Data moving from the Spreadsheet to the Database is pasted into separate fields in form view or list view. Works assumes that one row in the Spreadsheet represents one record in the Database.

Field entries moving from list view to the Spreadsheet are pasted, one entry per cell, into equivalent rows and columns.

LINKING DATA

When you link spreadsheet data or charts to a document created with the Word Processor, Works can update the copy automatically whenever you edit the source document. Links don't disappear when you close a file or quit Works because the program records, for each linked file, where and how the file is linked to other documents.

To keep your links current, Works asks whether you want to update them whenever you open a linked file. And whenever you close the file, Works asks whether you want to save the record.

Linking Spreadsheets

To link spreadsheet data to a word processed document,

1. If necessary, save the spreadsheet. This is important because Works will not create links from an unsaved document.

2. Highlight the cells you want to link and copy them to the Clipboard. If you copy a formula, Works copies the calculated value and updates the value in the word processed document whenever you edit or recalculate the formula in the Spreadsheet.

3. If it's not already open, open the receiving document in the Word Processor. Move the insertion point to the place where you want the linked information to appear.

4. Choose Paste Special from the Edit menu. When you're linking spreadsheet data, you see the following dialog box. Notice that the Paste Link button, which creates the link, is dimmed.

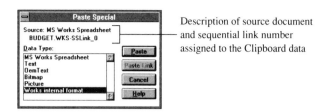

Description of source document and sequential link number assigned to the Clipboard data

5. In the Data Type list box, click MS Works Spreadsheet to activate the Paste Link button. Click Paste Link; a few seconds later the linked data appears in your word processed document.

When you've created a link, you can return to the source spreadsheet in either of the following ways:

■ Double-click the linked data in the word processed document.

■ Highlight the linked data and choose Edit MS Works Spreadsheet Object from the Word Processor's Edit menu.

Linking Charts

Linking a chart is even easier than linking spreadsheet data:

1. Open the spreadsheet from which the chart was created.

2. Place the insertion point where you want the chart to appear in the word processed document.

3. Choose Chart from the Word Processor's Insert menu. The following dialog box appears:

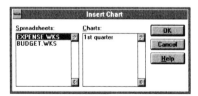

Highlight the spreadsheet you want in the list box headed Spreadsheets, click the chart you want in the list that appears in the Charts box, and click OK. A few seconds later, the chart you selected appears in your document.

To edit a linked chart,

1. Open the spreadsheet to which it belongs.

2. Double-click on the linked copy in your word processed document.

Editing Links

The Links command on the Edit menu lets you work with links themselves rather than with your linked data. You use the Links command to change the way Works updates the copy, from automatic updating to manual ("only on command"). You also use it to remove links, and—importantly—to redefine a link when you change the name or storage location of the source document.

When you choose the Links command, this dialog box appears:

- The Links box displays the links in your current document, listing both the source documents and the link numbers Works has assigned. To edit a link, highlight the one you want to change.

- Click Manual if you want to decide when to update links.

- Click the Update Now button to update your links.

- Click the Cancel Link button to remove a highlighted link.

- Click the Change Link button to rename a link. Change Link produces the following dialog box. Choose the drive, directory, or filename you need to describe the new name or location of your source document, and then click OK.

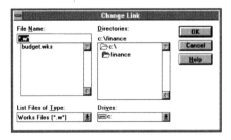

- Click Play or Edit (in the Links dialog box) to run the source application. Play starts the application; Edit opens the application for editing.

EMBEDDING OBJECTS

Chapter 5, which was devoted to Microsoft Draw, was actually all about embedded objects—drawings that you create in Draw but use in a word processed document. In addition to drawings, you can also embed spreadsheet data, notes produced by the Works Note-It utility, and information from other Windows programs that support embedding.

NOTE: *Entertaining as it can be, Note-It is not described in detail here because it is simple to use and comes with its own Help. To request help, choose Note-It from the Insert menu and click Help in the dialog box that appears.*

To create an embedded object,

1. Open a document in the Works Word Processor, and place the insertion point where you want the object to appear.

2. Choose the Object command from the Insert menu. A dialog box like this appears:

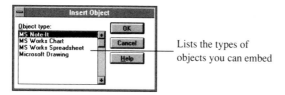

Lists the types of objects you can embed

The items on the Object Type list depend on what programs you have installed and whether they support embedded objects, but at a minimum you should see MS Note-It, MS Works Chart, MS Works Spreadsheet, and Microsoft Drawing—all objects related to Works itself.

3. Click the type of object you want and click OK.

When Works carries out the command, it starts the application that creates the object. When you finish creating the note, picture, or document you want to embed, finish up in one of the following ways:

■ If you've created a note in the Note-It dialog box, click OK.

■ If you've created a Works spreadsheet, choose Update from the File menu. Use the Window menu to return to your word processed document.

■ If you've created a Draw object, choose Exit And Return. Click Yes when Draw asks whether you want to update the word processed document.

■ If you've created an object with an application other than Works, choose whichever command is comparable to Update or Exit And Return. If you have questions about what to do, refer to your manual or, if the application provides it, check the online Help.

To edit an embedded object, double-click on it or choose Edit *objecttype* Object from the Word Processor's Edit menu.

NOTE: *The Edit...Object command applies to both linked and embedded objects, including drawings. The command is normally dimmed and appears simply as Object on the Edit menu. When you select a linked or embedded object, however, the command name changes to describe the type of object you highlighted. For example, if you highlight a Draw object, the command reads Edit Microsoft Drawing Object.*

If you're not sure whether to link or embed spreadsheet data, choose linking if you want to be sure that your data is always up-to-date. Choose embedding for less vital data or for introducing ''text'' that is easier to organize or format in the Spreadsheet—numbers, for example, or simple tables. If you use embedded numbers or tables, here's a tip: You probably don't want gridlines, so get rid of them before embedding your data by turning the lines off with the Show Gridlines command on the Options menu in the Spreadsheet.

CREATING CUSTOMIZED MAILINGS

Creating customized mailings—personalized form letters—involves merging two types of document: a database of names and addresses, and a word processed letter. You can create form letters with the Address Books and Form Letters WorksWizards, or you can create them on your own. Using the WorksWizards adds the recipient's name and address and an optional salutation at the top of the letter. Creating form letters

Going Beyond the Letter

Even though this section emphasizes form letters, you needn't stop with them. To Works, a form letter is nothing more than a word processed document into which you insert information from database fields. It doesn't matter that your ''letter'' is, in fact, a catalog, an inventory list, or an invoice, so let your imagination run free and think ''form letter'' whenever you have to customize a boilerplate document with database specifics.

on your own lets you insert personal information elsewhere, within the body of the letter. Either way, the process is not difficult.

Mailing Lists

A mailing list is a simple database containing names and addresses. You can create one in the Database, using the procedures described in Chapter 8, or you can automate the process with the Address Books Works-Wizard. Of the two methods, the Address Books WorksWizard is easier and more foolproof, especially if you want to use the Form Letters WorksWizard too. The reason: The Form Letters WorksWizard looks specifically—and only—for field names built into its Address Books companion.

If you create a mailing list on your own and want to use it with the Form Letters WorksWizard, be sure that your field names exactly match those in the Address Books WorksWizard, right down to capitalization, spacing, and punctuation. Works, of course, doesn't expect you to know or remember precisely what these fields are, so it provides you an easy way to check:

1. Choose Open Existing File from the File menu.
2. Choose FIELDS.WPS from the MSWORKS directory. The beginning of the file looks like this:

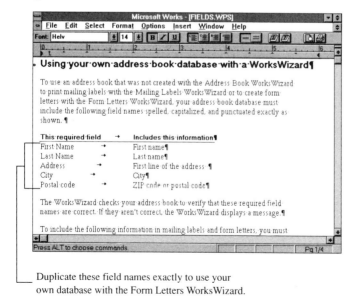

Duplicate these field names exactly to use your own database with the Form Letters WorksWizard.

Form Letters

Once you've created your database, the next step is to work on the letter or other document you want to customize. If you're planning to use the Form Letters WorksWizard, write the body of the document first. The WorksWizard helps you customize the document, not write it.

To use the Form Letters WorksWizard, begin by opening the database and word processed document you need. (Opening the documents ahead of time isn't necessary, but it can save a few moments of your time.) Once you start the WorksWizard, you're guided through the entire process, and you're given the opportunity to show the WorksWizard where to place the name, address, and salutation. As it customizes your letter, the WorksWizard inserts field names as *placeholders* for your data. The following illustration shows such placeholders at the top of a letter:

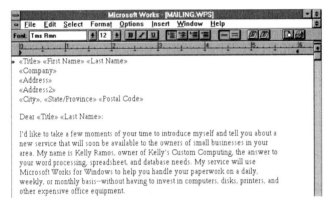

When the letter is complete, choose the WorksWizard option that allows you to exit and print the letters. This option quits the WorksWizard and returns you to the Word Processor, so choose it even if you've noticed that the document needs some extra formatting or other fine-tuning. Back in the Word Processor, make any necessary adjustments; when you're ready to print the letters,

1. Choose Print Form Letters (not Print) from the File menu.

2. In the dialog box that appears, highlight the correct database if it's not already highlighted and, unless you're certain the letters will print correctly, choose Preview.

NOTE: *It's important to choose Print Form Letters because this command tells Works to replace database field names with the actual entries they represent in a process known as* merge printing. *If you choose Print instead, Works doesn't fold the database information into the word processed document. It simply prints the document, complete with field names.*

Inserting database fields

If you don't want to use the Form Letters WorksWizard, you can easily insert database fields as placeholders for data anywhere you want in a word processed document. Use this approach if you want to

- Use a mailing list with field names that don't match those created by the Address Books WorksWizard

- Create a "form letter" that is really some other type of document

- Insert customized information within the body of the letter or document

To insert field names in a word processed document,

1. Move the insertion point to the location at which you want the field name to appear.

2. Choose Database Field from the Insert menu. Provide the necessary information in the resulting dialog box, and then click OK:

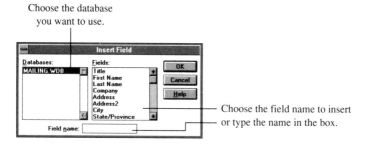

Choose the database you want to use.

Choose the field name to insert or type the name in the box.

Repeat the same steps for each field name you want to insert in your document. When you're ready to print, choose Print Form Letters from the File menu, as described above.

Mailing Labels

As long as you have a database of names and addresses, you can print sheets of mailing labels. To set up the labels, you can either use the Mailing Labels WorksWizard or perform for yourself the simple steps listed on the next page.

1. In the Word Processor, use the Database Field command on the Insert menu to create a simple "label" document that consists of place-holders for the fields you want to print, as shown below. (Note the spaces and punctuation where needed.)

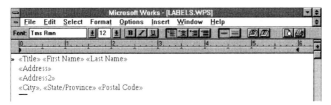

2. Save the document and open the database you need.

3. Choose Print Labels from the File menu. In the resulting dialog box, specify the database and the necessary measurements:

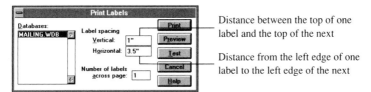

Distance between the top of one label and the top of the next

Distance from the left edge of one label to the left edge of the next

4. Click Preview to see how the labels will print, or click Test to print two test rows of labels. To print the labels, click the Print button. Works displays the Page Setup & Margins dialog box so you can make the proper adjustments. When you're satisfied, click OK to print the labels.

Envelopes

You can print envelopes using much the same procedure as the one de-scribed for mailing labels. Because envelopes and printers vary in their capabilities, however, you might need to refer to your printer manual for instructions on feeding single envelopes or using an envelope bin. You'll also probably have to do some experimenting with the Page Setup & Margins command.

For single envelopes,

■ Create an "envelope" document by inserting the database fields you need. Use the Indents & Spacing and the Page Setup & Margins com-mands to specify the correct envelope length and width, indents, and spacing. Use the Print Form Letters command to print the envelopes.

For formfeed envelopes,

■ Set up a similar document, but as a "mailing label." Use the Indents & Spacing command to indent the recipient's address. Then use the Print Labels command to specify the correct horizontal and vertical spacing. When you print, narrow the margins and type the correct envelope length and width.

NOTE: *During printing, if Works tells you there's a mismatch between page setup and the paper size specified in the Printer Setup command, click Continue to override the complaint.*

APPENDIX A

Installing Works

If you have Works, you presumably have a suitable computer on which to run it. For reference, however, the following list tells you the basic hardware and software requirements for running Works:

- A computer with an 80286 or higher microprocessor
- Optimally, 1 megabyte (fairly standard on new computers) or more of memory
- At least one floppy-disk drive
- A hard disk
- An EGA, VGA, 8514/A, Hercules Graphics, or compatible video graphics adapter supported by Microsoft Windows; recommended (and enjoyable): a color adapter
- MS-DOS version 3.1 or later
- Microsoft Windows version 3.0 or later
- Not required but recommended: a mouse

NOTE: *Before you can install Works, you must have installed Windows, so refer to your Windows manual if Windows does not start on your computer.*

Installing Works is a breeze, even if you've never installed a software product before:

1. Start your computer and Windows. If an onscreen window titled Program Manager does not open, press the Ctrl and Esc keys at the same time to display a small window titled Task List.

   Point to the words *Program Manager* with your mouse and double-click (click twice in succession). If you don't have a mouse, use the arrow keys to move the dark highlight to Program Manager. Then press Tab so that a dotted box moves to the button labeled Switch To, and press Enter.

2. Find the Works disk that has the word *Setup* on it, and place the disk in one of your floppy-disk drives. (Most people use drive A, although either will do.)

3. If you have a mouse, point to the menu name *File* at the top of the Program Manager window and click once. (If you don't have a mouse, hold down Alt and press the F key.)

4. With the mouse, point to *Run* on the menu and click once. (With the keyboard, press the R key.)

5. When a box labeled *Run* appears on the screen, type the letter of the drive containing your Setup disk, a colon, and the word *setup*. If your disk is in drive A, the command looks like this:

   `a:setup`

   If the disk is in drive B, the command is

   `b:setup`

6. Click OK or press the Tab key and then press Enter to carry out the command.

In a few moments, the screen fills with the opening Setup screen. From this point on, follow the instructions Setup displays. It begins by asking you to type your name and, optionally, the name of your company. After that, aside from asking whether you want a complete or a custom installation (choose complete), Setup charges ahead on its own, stopping periodically only to ask you to insert a different disk.

When the installation is over, Setup will display a screen giving you the choice of returning to Windows or starting Works. Make whichever choice you want. Works is now on your hard disk, ready for work.

Works Functions

Works includes 57 built-in functions you can use instead of defining your own formulas to do the same work. Every function has a name and must be typed in the following format:

`=FUNCTIONNAME(Argument0,Argument1,...ArgumentN)`

- The equal sign (=) tells Works you are entering a function/formula to be calculated.

- FUNCTIONNAME is the name of the function. Function names are shown in all capital letters in the following descriptions.

- *Argument0,Argument1,...ArgumentN* represent arguments—values— to be used in the calculation. Arguments can be numbers, cell references, range references, range names, field names, or other functions, but they *must* represent numbers. For example, if cell B3 is included as an argument, B3 must contain a numeric value.

- Arguments, if used, are always enclosed in parentheses. If a function takes multiple arguments, they must be separated by commas. If a function takes no arguments, FUNCTIONNAME must be followed by an empty set of parentheses—for example, NOW( ).

The following descriptions provide an alphabetic reference to the Works functions. For ease of reference, trigonometric and other mathematical functions are grouped under the heading "Math Functions"; functions related to the clock and calendar are grouped under "Time and Date Functions."

ABS(x)
Gives the absolute value of *x*, a positive or negative number.

ACOS, ASIN, ATAN, ATAN2. See Math Functions.

AVG(range0, range1,... rangeN)
Averages all the values in the ranges listed as arguments. *Range0, range1,...rangeN* can be numbers, cell or range references, or formulas.

Text within a range is always treated as 0, as are blank cells if they occur in cell references. Blank cells in range references are ignored.

CHOOSE(x,option0,option1,...optionN)

Uses the value of x to tell you the value of the option whose position in the list of arguments corresponds to x. For example,

```
=CHOOSE(2,30,60,90,120)
```

returns 90, because its position (starting from 0) corresponds to 2 in the list of options.

COLS(range)

Gives the number of columns in a range, such as A1:C1, specified by *range*. See also ROWS.

COS. See Math Functions.

COUNT(range0,range1,...rangeN)

Gives the number of cells in the ranges specified. The function arguments *range0,range1,...rangeN* can be numbers, cell or range references, or formulas. COUNT counts cells containing numbers, text, and the values ERR and N/A, which are returned by other functions. Blank cells are counted only if they occur in individual cell (not range) references.

CTERM(interest rate,future value,present value)

Calculates the number of compounding periods required for an investment to grow from *present value* to *future value*, given a fixed *interest rate* per compounding period.

NOTE: *The interest rate is for a single compounding period. For rates representing more than one period, divide the interest rate by the frequency (such as monthly) at which the interest is compounded. Type the rate as a percent (12%) or as a decimal value (.12).*

Date and Time Functions

The date and time functions help you convert to and from calculable serial numbers and familiar, "readable" dates and times. Arguments in the time and date functions are as follows:

- *year*: a four-digit number such as 1992 or a number from 0 (for 1900) through 179 (for 2079)
- *month*: a number from 1 through 12
- *day*: a number from 1 through 31

- *date*: a serial number between 1 and 65534, representing dates from 1/1/1900 through 6/3/2079

- *time*: a serial number between 0 and 0.99999, representing 12 AM through 11:59:59 PM

- *hour*: a number from 0 through 23

- *minute* and *second*: for each, a number from 0 through 59

Function	Returns
DATE(*year,month,day*)	A date, such as =DATE(1992,12,25), converted to a serial number.
DAY(*date*) MONTH(*date*) YEAR(*date*)	The number of the day, month, or year of a date represented by *date*.
HOUR(*time*) MINUTE(*time*) SECOND(*time*)	The number of the hour, minute, or second of the time represented by *time*.
NOW()	A serial number representing the current date and time. The serial number is updated at each recalculation. You can use the Time/Date command to view the serial number as a time or date.
TIME(*hour,minute,second*)	A time converted to a serial number, which represents the hours, minutes, and seconds between 12:00:00 AM and 11:59:59 PM.

DDB(*cost,salvage,life,period*)

Uses the double declining balance method to calculate depreciation of an asset for a particular *period*. *Cost* is the original cost of the asset; *salvage* is the expected value at the end of the asset's life; *life* is the number of time periods the asset is expected to be usable.

The function calculates depreciation for a given period as (*value*$*2$)/*life*, where *value* represents the book value for that period (its cost diminished by any prior depreciation).

ERR()

Displays the value ERR in a cell; usually used to check for a specific condition, as in

```
=IF(A1<0,ERR(),A1)
```

where ERR appears if the value in cell A1 is less than 0. (See IF for an explanation of the IF function.)

EXP. See Math Functions.

FALSE()

Displays the value 0, meaning False, in a cell; usually used in a formula to check for errors or special conditions. For example,

`=IF(A1>0,TRUE(),FALSE())`

returns 1 (True) if the value in cell A1 is greater than 0, but 0 (False) if the value is 0 or less. See also TRUE, IF.

FV(*payment, rate, term*)

Calculates the future value of an annuity in which equal *payments* earn a fixed *rate* per term, compounded over the specified number of *terms*. The first payment is assumed to be made at the end of the first period, and future value is calculated as follows:

$$payment * ((1+rate)^{term} - 1)/rate$$

HLOOKUP(*search value, range, row*)

Uses a search value to retrieve an entry from a predefined table. *Search value* is a value in the top row of the table; *range* is the range of cells in the table; *row* is the number of rows down that the function searches for the desired entry. Search values in the top row should be in ascending order. In the following example, HLOOKUP returns the value 500:

=HLOOKUP(10,A1:C4,2)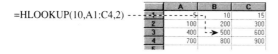

HLOOKUP always searches in the same pattern, across and then down, as illustrated. It returns 0 if the target cell contains text. See also VLOOKUP.

HOUR. See Date and Time Functions.

IF(*condition, true value, false value*)

Returns one of two results, depending on the outcome of a specified condition. *Condition* is the condition to evaluate and is often an expression that includes an operator such as > (greater than), < (less than), or = (equals); *true value* is the value that is displayed if the outcome of the condition is true; *false value* is displayed if the outcome of the condition is not true. IF functions can be nested, one inside the other, to refine the results of a conditional statement, as on the next page.

```
=IF(A1>1000,A1*10%,IF(A1>750,A1*8%,A1*6%))
```

This example can be translated as, "If the value in A1 is greater than 1000, multiply the value in A1 by 10%. If the value in A1 is greater than 750 (but less than 1001), multiply it by 8%. Otherwise, multiply the value in A1 by 6%."

INDEX(*range,column,row*)

Provides the value of the cell at the intersection of *column* and *row*. Column and row numbers begin with 0, so the intersection of column 0 and row 0 is the first value in *range*.

INT(*x*)

Gives the integer part of *x* without rounding up or down. For example, both =INT(3.14) and =INT(3.99) produce 3.

IRR(*guess,range*)

Calculates the internal rate of return (profit) on the series of values represented by *range*. *Guess* is an estimate of the yield; typically, a value between 0 and 1 is recommended as a starting point for *guess*. IRR uses a trial-and-error approach called iteration in which repeated calculations are used to refine the initial *guess*. If calculations do not produce a meaningful result within 20 iterations, the function displays ERR.

ISERR(*x*)

Determines whether *x* is the error value ERR. If yes, the function displays 1; otherwise, the function displays 0. ISERR can be used to control the propagation of the ERR error message through related formulas in a spreadsheet. For example, =IF(ISERR(C15),0,C15) displays 0 if cell C15 contains an error, but otherwise displays the value in cell C15.

ISNA(*x*)

Determines whether *x* is the value N/A (not available); similar to the ISERR function in helping prevent the propagation of one value (N/A) throughout related formulas in a spreadsheet.

LN, LOG. See Math Functions.

Math Functions

Works includes the following math and trigonometric functions. Arguments are defined within each description. Angle measurements, as arguments or as return values, are expressed in radians.

Function	Returns
ACOS(x)	Arccosine of an angle whose cosine is x
ASIN(x)	Arcsine of an angle whose sine is x
ATAN(x)	Arctangent of an angle whose tangent is x
ATAN2(x,y)	Arctangent of an angle defined by coordinates x and y
COS(x)	Cosine of an angle x
EXP(x)	Value of 2.71828..., the base of the natural logarithm, raised to the power of x
LN(x)	Natural logarithm, base e, to the power of x
LOG(x)	Base 10 logarithm of x
MOD(*num,denom*)	Remainder (modulus) of *num* (numerator) divided by *denom* (denominator)
PI( )	Value of pi (3.14159...)
SIN(x)	Sine of an angle x
SQRT(x)	Square root of x, a positive number
TAN(x)	Tangent of an angle x

MAX(*range0,range1,...rangeN*)
MIN(*range0,range1,...rangeN*)

Give, respectively, the largest (maximum) and smallest (minimum) values in the referenced ranges. *Range0,range1,...rangeN* can be numbers, cell or range references, or formulas. Both functions ignore blank cells in range references but treat them as 0 in cell references.

MINUTE. See Date and Time Functions.

MOD. See Math Functions.

MONTH. See Date and Time Functions.

NA()

Produces the value N/A (not available). Works treats N/A as a numeric, not a text, value. See also ISNA.

NOW. See Date and Time Functions.

NPV(*rate,range*)

Calculates the net present value of a series of payments in *range* at a fixed interest *rate* per period. If the interest rate is annual, but the payment periods are more frequent, divide the rate by the number of periods (such as 12). The range can include a number of cells, but must cover no more than one row or column.

NPV assumes that payments occur at the end of periods of equal length and calculates the result as

$$\sum_{i=1}^{n} \frac{Payment\,[i]}{(1 + Rate)\,i}$$

PI. See Math Functions.

PMT(*principal,rate,term*)

Calculates the payment per period on a loan or investment represented by *principal* at a fixed interest rate per period over the specified *term*. *Rate* and *term* must correspond to the same periods. If the rate is annual but payment is monthly, divide the rate by 12. The function assumes that payments are made at the end of each period and calculates the result as follows:

present value $*$ *rate*$/(1 - (1 + rate)^{-term})$

PV(*payment,rate,term*)

Calculates the present value of a series of equal *payments* earning a fixed *rate* of interest over a specified *term*. The function assumes that the first payment is made at the end of the first period. The calculation (for rates not equal to 0) is based on the expression below. See also NPV, which calculates the net present value.

payment $*$ $(1 - (1 + rate)^{-term})/rate$

RAND()

Returns a random number, which is a decimal fraction from 0 up to, but not including, 1.

RATE(*future value,present value,term*)

Returns the fixed interest rate per period needed for an investment to grow from its *present value* to an expected *future value* in the number of terms specified. The result is calculated as follows:

$(future\ value/present\ value)^{1/term} - 1$

ROUND(*x,places*)

Rounds the value x to the number of *places* specified. If *places* is 0, the function rounds the value to the nearest integer; if *places* is positive, the function rounds to the right of the decimal point; if *places* is negative, the function rounds to the left of the decimal.

ROWS(*range*)

Returns the number of rows in *range*. See also COLS.

SECOND. See Date and Time Functions.

SIN. See Math Functions.

SLN(*cost,salvage,life*)

Calculates the straight-line depreciation for an asset. Straight-line depreciation assumes a linear reduction in value, so the depreciation amount is the same for any period. *Cost* is the initial cost of the asset; *salvage* is its estimated salvage value; *life* is the number of periods the asset is expected to remain useful. The result is calculated as *cost − salvage/life*.

SQRT. See Math Functions.

STD(*range0,range1,...rangeN*)

Calculates the population standard deviation of the values in the specified ranges. *Range0,range1,...rangeN* can be numbers, cell or range references, or formulas. Blank cells are ignored in range references but are treated as 0 in cell references. To calculate the standard deviation of a sample, use the following formula:

```
STD(ranges)*SQRT(COUNT(ranges)/(COUNT(ranges)-1))
```

where *ranges* includes *range0,range1,...rangeN* for the functions involved.

SUM(*range0,range1,...rangeN*)

Totals the values in the specified ranges. *Range0,range1,...rangeN* can be numbers, cell references or ranges, or formulas. Blank cells are ignored in range references and treated as 0 in cell references.

SYD(*cost,salvage,life,period*)

Calculates depreciation of an asset according to the sum-of-the-years-digits method, in which the greatest allowances for depreciation are made in the earliest years in the life of the asset. *Cost* is the initial cost of the asset; *salvage* is the estimated salvage value of the asset; *life* is the estimated useful life of the asset; *period* is the period for which depreciation is to be calculated. The calculation is based on the following formula:

$$(cost − salvage)*(life − period + 1)/(life*(life +1)/2)$$

TAN. See Math Functions.

TERM(*payment,rate,future value*)

Calculates the number of periods required for an annuity to grow to the specified *future value* at a fixed interest *rate* and a fixed *payment* per period. If the interest rate is annual, divide the rate by 12 for a monthly payment period.

TIME. See Date and Time Functions.

TRUE()

Displays the value 1, meaning True, in a cell; usually used in other formulas to check for errors or special conditions. See also FALSE.

VAR(*range0,range1,...rangeN*)

Calculates variance—the degree to which the values in the specified ranges deviate from the mean for all values. *Range0,range1,...rangeN* can be numbers, cell or range references, or formulas. Blank cells are ignored in range references and treated as 0 in cell references. To calculate sample variance, use the following formula:

```
VAR(ranges)*(COUNT(ranges)/(COUNT(ranges)-1))
```

where *ranges* includes *range0,range1,...rangeN* as described above.

VLOOKUP(*search value,range,column*)

Uses a search value to retrieve an entry from a predefined table. *Search value* is a value in the leftmost column of the table; *range* is the range of cells in the table; *column* is the number of columns that the function searches to the right to retrieve the desired entry. Search values in the leftmost column should be in ascending order.

=VLOOKUP(10,A1:C4,2) - -

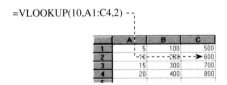

VLOOKUP always searches in the same pattern, down and then across, as illustrated. It returns 0 if the target cell contains text. See also HLOOKUP.

YEAR. See Date and Time Functions.

Index

Numbers in *italics* refer to figures or tables.

Special Characters

" (quotation marks), 95, 155
$ (dollar sign), 94, 99, 144
& (AND operator), 100, 101, 156–57
( ) (parentheses), 101
* (asterisk as multiplication operator), 100, 101, 156
* (asterisk as wildcard character), 152
+ (addition operator), 100, 101, 156
– (subtraction operator), 100, 101, 156
... (ellipsis), *14*
/ (division operator), 100, 101, 156
: (colon), 90
< (less-than operator), 100, 101, 155
<= (less-than-or-equal-to operator), 100, 101, 155
<> (not-equal-to operator), 100, 101, 155
= (equal sign), 97, 100, 101, 148, 155, 190
> (greater-than operator), 100, 101, 155
>= (greater-than-or-equal-to operator), 100, 101, 155
? (wildcard character), 152
\ (backslash), 11, 12
^ (exponentiation operator), 100, 101, 156
| (OR operator), 100, 101, 156–57
~ (NOT operator), 100, 101

A–B

ABS function, 190
absolute cell references, 99
ACOS function, 195
active window, xii
addition operator (+), 100, 101, 156
Address Books WorksWizard, 21, 182, 183
aligning
    database field entries, 145–46
    document text, 55–56
    fields on database forms, 136
    spreadsheet cell contents, 95, 108
ampersand (&), 100, 101, 156–57
AND operator (&), 100, 101, 156–57
applications, cutting and pasting between, 176–77
application software, defined, vii
application window, xi, xii, xiv, 32
Arc tool, 75
arguments, 190
arranging windows, 33–35
Arrow tool, 73
ASIN function, 195
asterisk (*)
    as multiplication operator, 100, 101, 156
    as wildcard character, 152
ATAN2 function, 195
ATAN function, 195

Autosum button, 98
AVG function, 190–91
axes, 116, 117, 118, 128–30
Back button (WorksWizards), 21
backslash (\), 11, 12
Backspace key, 48
backup copies, 24
bar charts, 115, 118–19
    adding data labels to, 125–26
    patterns and colors for, 127–28
    selecting values for, 116–17
Bar dialog box, 118–19, 124
blocks, text. *See* paragraphs
boilerplate. *See* templates
boldfacing
    in databases, 145–46
    in documents, 54
    in spreadsheets, 107–8
bookmarks, in Help, 40
Borders command, 108
Bring to Front command, 83
buttons, *xii*, xv–xvi, 16

C

C:\>, viii
calculations. *See also* field summaries
    in database field entries, 147
    in database queries, 156
    in database reports, 162, 164, 168–69, 170–71
    order of evaluation in, 100–101
    in spreadsheets, 97–101
    using Autosum button, 98
Cancel box, 92, 135
caret (^), 100, 101, 156
Cascade command, 34
categories, 116
category labels, 116
cell references, 89, 98–99
cells, 6, 88–89
    aligning, 95, 108
    copying contents, 104, 105
    dates and times in, 89
    deleting contents, 104–5
    editing contents, 102
    entering data in, 91–92
    filling series of, 95–97
    finding, 111
    formatting, 93–95, 107–8
    formulas in, 89
    inserting data from Clipboard, 105–6
    jumping to, 110–11

JoAnne Woodcock

Currently a master writer for Microsoft Press, JoAnne Woodcock is author of *Microsoft Works for Windows* and the *Concise Guide to MS-DOS 5.0,* coauthor of *Running Unix* and *Microsoft Word Style Sheets,* and contributor to the *Microsoft Press Computer Dictionary,* all published by Microsoft Press.

The manuscript for this book was prepared and submitted to Microsoft Press in electronic form. Text files were processed and formatted using Microsoft Word.

Principal editorial compositor: Barb Runyan
Principal proofreader: Kathleen Atkins
Principal typographer: Ruth Pettis
Interior text designer: Kim Eggleston
Principal illustrator: Lisa Sandburg
Cover designer: Rikki Conrad Design
Cover color separator: Color Service

Text composition by Microsoft Press in Times Roman with display type in Futura Heavy, using the Magna composition system and the Linotronic 300 laser imagesetter.

Printed on recycled paper stock.